BONKERS BOOKS

THINK of a LINK

how to REMEMBER absolutely EVERYTHING

WRITTEN BY

Andy Salmon

Illustrated by Clive Goddard

SCHOLASTIC

For Alex, Freddie, Lulu and Alexander.

Scholastic Children's Books,
Euston House, 24 Eversholt Street,
London, NW1 1DB, UK

A division of Scholastic Ltd
London ~ New York ~ Toronto ~ Sydney ~ Auckland
Mexico City ~ New Delhi ~ Hong Kong

First published in the UK by Scholastic Ltd, 2011

Text copyright © Andy Salmon 2011
Illustration copyright © Clive Goddard, 2011
All rights reserved

ISBN 978 1407 116 488
Printed and bound in the UK by CPI Mackays, Chatham ME5 8TD

2 4 6 8 10 9 7 5 3 1

FORGOTTEN THE CAPITAL OF TURKEY
OR SPAIN?

OR WHAT LANGUAGE THEY SPEAK IN
PERU OR BAHRAIN?

WHO'S ON THE BACK OF A
TEN-POUND NOTE?

OR HOW MANY PLAYS OLD
SHAKESPEARE WROTE?

WHAT WAS INVENTED BY
TIM BERNERS-LEE?

WHICH RIVER FLOWS INTO THE
CASPIAN SEA?

DON'T WRITE ALL THIS DOWN WITH
INDELIBLE INK.

JUST REMEMBER IT ALL BY THINKING
OF A LINK!

CONTENTS

INTRODUCTION

Have you ever DREAMED of REMEMBERING absolutely everything in the whole wide world? Every capital city, every date, every KING and QUEEN, every meaning of every word, every spelling, and even every type of chocolate bar you've ever heard of? Wouldn't it be so SATISFYING to put your HAND UP IN CLASS before the school boff, Nigel Know-It-All?

Pah! That's just boring memorizing stuff. I don't want to remember everything off by heart — and anyway my brain would explode!

Well, actually it wouldn't. Your brain is designed to remember more information than you can possibly imagine. Did you know that your brain can store EVERYTHING you experience, see, read or hear? Mind-blowing but true! The trick is being able to recall all these facts when you need to. And that's where linking comes in.

What is linking?

Here's a fact for you: Budapest is the capital of the European country Hungary.

If you want to remember this, you'll need to try to think of a link that permanently connects Budapest and Hungary in your mind. If you can, it'll mean that the next time you hear Hungary, you'll immediately think of Budapest and the other way round. Here's a link that may work for you:

*Is my **hungry bud**(dy) **a pest** or what?*

(Hungry – sounds like Hungary.)

If this doesn't tickle your fancy, then try to think of your own. It's fun to think of your own links because they mean more to you and that makes them easier to remember. It doesn't matter if your creation doesn't work for anyone else. If it works for you, it works! The cherry on the cake is if someone else uses your link to recall a particular fact.

Linking is like a fairground ride that never ends, and the great thing is you don't need a ticket. All that's required is a brain, an imagination and the ability to laugh a lot. Your guide for this oh-so-exciting adventure is me, Sir Linkalot.

There are many ways to link. Here are a few different techniques you can try:

RHYMING LINKS

Rhyming makes it easier to remember a fact. Here's a nice rhyming couplet to help you recall that Guy Fawkes's unsuccessful Gunpowder Plot was on 5 November 1605:

There was a BANG at the door at five past four.

Five past four in the afternoon, or 4.05 pm, can be written as 16:05 in 24-hour clock time. And '05' also links to the fifth day of November.

If you want to know that King James I (a Scot) was the monarch at the time, then see if this link lights your fire:

*King James the Scot
didn't like flames a lot.*

SIR LINKALOT'S WARNING

Using a rhyme to remember a fact is a handy technique. But beware, my linking wannabe. The rhyme needs to be catchy and not too long, so you can recall it with ease. Otherwise you will have to learn two things, the fact and the rhyme! So use them with caution.

ACROSTIC LINKS

An acrostic (a cross tick: A X ✓) is where you make a sentence out of the first letter of each word of the thing you want to remember or each letter of a word you want to remember.

a. Spelling example

The word 'future' can be misspelled in two or three different places. This is where an acrostic comes into its own, because it includes every letter.

<u>F</u>reshen <u>u</u>p <u>t</u>he <u>u</u>niverse. <u>R</u>ecycle <u>e</u>verything.

If you make the acrostic relevant
to the thing you want to learn,
it'll be even more memorable.

b. Sequence example

The order of the planets, starting with the nearest to the Sun, is:

<u>M</u>ercury <u>V</u>enus <u>E</u>arth <u>M</u>ars <u>J</u>upiter <u>S</u>aturn <u>U</u>ranus <u>N</u>eptune

(Tiny Pluto was once known as a 'planet', but it was renamed a 'dwarf planet' in 2006.)

<u>M</u>y <u>V</u>ery <u>E</u>normous <u>M</u>onster <u>J</u>ust <u>S</u>ucked <u>U</u>p <u>N</u>eptune.[1]

Note that Mercury and Mars could be mixed up. Just remember that 'My' and 'Mercury' begin and end with the same letters.

Linking facts to a famous person or thing is a sure-fire way of remembering something. If you can think of a link that's connected to Doctor Who, Indiana Jones, James Bond, or even Coca-Cola then there's more chance of recalling it, as these well-known things are already in your memory banks.

FACT: <u>Swimming</u> is one of the words 8-11 year olds misspell most often.

The tricky part is remembering how many Ms there are. When I see two Ms together, I think of the following:

Millimetres, M&M's sweets, Mickey Mouse, Eminem (the rapper), the Millenium (the year 2000 in Roman numerals is MM, because M = 1000)...

M&M's are close to my heart, so let's use that one:

<u>M&M</u>'s are swi<u>mm</u>ing in calories.

Linking the thing you need to learn to a favourite fact in your memory banks is a <u>sweet</u> idea.

A lot of people find that using an image is a good way to remember things. For example, the spelling of 'their' and 'there' is often mixed up because these words sound the same. But they are spelled differently and mean different things: 'their' is about belonging, whereas 'there' is about place. A simple image can help tell them apart:

This linking technique is particularly useful when spelling, because the next time you write these two words, you are sort of copying this image stored in your memory. Letters are pictures, after all!

14

STORY LINKS

Are you sitting comfortably? Then I'll begin…

If you need to remember a list of things or a whole bunch of facts in one go, then story linking is the solution to all your problems.

FACT 1: Mount Everest is the world's highest mountain.

FACT 2: It's in the country Nepal.

FACT 3: Sir Edmund Hillary and the Sherpa mountaineer guide Tenzing were the first to climb it.

Let's link these facts by putting them into a short story:

I need to <u>Everest</u> as I've a <u>Nepalling</u> stitch and my legs are <u>Tenzing</u> up. This mountain is a lot more <u>Hillary</u> than I envisaged.

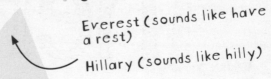

Everest (sounds like have a rest)

Hillary (sounds like hilly)

Remembering a story is far easier than learning individual facts. It's a good idea if you try to think of your own story – if you've made it up, it'll be even easier to remember.

15

LETTER LINKS

Have I got some exciting news for you? Letter linking is about to put an end to your spelling issues, for ever!

Spelling isn't easy, especially when new words are popping up all the time. Recently, the English language acquired its millionth word. Now that's a lot of linking to think of!

More often than not, there is just one 'killer' letter that makes people misspell a word.

Letter linking is using a familiar word or expression to help you spell a word. This is the formula:

(tricky word to spell) + (easier word to spell)
+ (familiar expression) = tricky word spelt!

Here are a couple of examples:

The 'w' of 'wrist', the 'g' of 'gnome' and the 'b' of 'comb' are all silent letters. Letter links help to remind you of this.

Wrist: <u>W</u>rist<u>w</u>atch
Gnome: <u>G</u>arden <u>g</u>nome
Comb: <u>B</u>rush and com<u>b</u>

Garden gnome

Wristwatch

Brush and comb

So the next time you hear the word 'wrist', you need to strap it on to the word watch.

There's no limit to letter linking. It can also work for multiple letters.

Biscuit: a) <u>Cu</u>p of tea and a bis<u>cu</u>it
          b) <u>Cu</u>stard cream bis<u>cu</u>it.

Surprise: B<u>urp</u>! That s<u>urp</u>rised me.

Exaggerate: You need to ex<u>agge</u>rate to st<u>agge</u>r me.

Numbers exist to help us with many things, including linking.

a) What's in a word?

Many numbers look like letters.

1 = I
2 = Z
3 = E (backwards)
4 = A
5 = S
6 = b or G
7 = J or Y
8 = B
9 = g
0 = O

So when you need to remember a fact, give these a whirl and see what you come up with. Number linking is an extremely useful technique.

For example, the word 'possesses' is riddled with Ss. Five of them, to be precise. So:

Po55e55e5 has 5 Ss.

b) I've got your number!

When you have to remember a fact that has a number in it, try linking the number to a well-known name or expression. It'll become much more interesting, making it easier to recall than a number standing on its lonesome.

FACT: India is the seventh biggest country in the world.

When I hear the number seven, I think of:

Seven wonders of the world, seven days of the week, seven dwarfs, 7 Up, James Bond – 007, seven seas (as in 'sail the seven seas'), lucky seven, seven-a-side...

Try this one for size:

Who's the <u>biggest</u> action hero, <u>India</u>na Jones or James Bond, 00<u>7</u>?

Numbers are all around us in many
shapes and sizes.
Linking creates more solutions and
a lot fewer surprises.

Linking good pun

A play on words is called a pun which, conveniently, rhymes with fun! Even SHAKESPEARE was a pun-master and you can't argue with the Great Bard himself!

Toe-curlingly cheesy 'you have to be kidding me' jokes can be useful. The reason why people never forget a good (or a bad) joke is that something that made you laugh (or groan) gets placed right at the front of your memory banks. We all want to remember things that make us smile.

It doesn't matter to me if it's a clever play on words or a crow-barred, corny rib-tickler. Basically, if it curls those lips up, then I'm a happy knight.

FACT: An aviary is a bird enclosure.

*Let's have a **hoot** trying to remember this...*

Aviary *day, I wake up to* **birds** *singing.*

*Wordplay is such good fun, or should that be **bird**-play?*

*I think I need to stop **lark**ing about before I go **stork** **raven** mad.*

SIR LINKALOT'S TIP

You can use more than one type
of link at a time.

Let me run this one by you...

21

Diarrhoea is a very difficult word to spell, with the middle bit 'rrho' being the sticky part. We can register a good score on the chuckle-o-meter here by using an acrostic, some humour and a visual aid. And see if you can spot the word 'poop'!

_R_unny, _r_unny, _h_elp ... _o_ops!

SIR LINKALOT'S WARNING

Only use an acrostic for the tricky part of the word, because the longer the acrostic, the harder it is to remember.

The Laws of LINKING

All you need to remember about linking is:

* Anyone can play.

* It makes learning fun, and the more fun you have, the easier you'll find it to remember things.

* There is always more than one solution. Try to find your own connections because if it's meaningful to you, it'll stick better.

In this book, you will discover loads of ready-made links to help you remember bundles of fascinating facts, such as ... the capital of Australia ... the inventor of the Internet ... the Roman god of the sea ... the year of the Great Fire of London ... the Fahrenheit equivalent to 25 degrees Celsius ... the wettest place on Earth ... and lots, lots more!

If you can think of a link for any of these facts, please send it to www.thinkalink.co.uk where you'll find out even more about the world of linking, and lots more brilliant links.

I must say a huge thank you to those who have already contributed their creations, many of which will be seen throughout this book. This is what the website is all about. All I, Sir Linkalot, am doing is kickstarting the whole process.

Welcome to the world of linking!

[1] This link was created by Keith Casson, Kent.

[2] This link was created by Barbara Yandell, Leicester.

THE 12 CHINESE NEW YEARS

The Chinese New Year is the most important of the traditional Chinese holidays and is commonly called the 'Lunar New Year' because it's based on the cycles of the Moon. A Chinese New Year usually falls on the second new Moon after the winter solstice. This can occur any time between 21 January and 20 February. A complete cycle takes 60 years and is made up of five 12-year cycles. Each of the years in a cycle is named after an animal. Legend has it that the animal ruling the year in which a person is born has a huge influence on his or her personality.

If you can learn this 12-year cycle, you'll be able to work out which animal rules in any one year! Just keep adding or taking away 12. For example, the Dragon ruled in 2000. So 1988 (2000 - 12) and 2012 (2000 + 12) are also Years of the Dragon.

2000 – Dragon

A dragon's
smoke rings: 0...0...0

2001 – Snake

A **wiggly 1** looks like a **snake**.

2002 – Horse

I'm **2 hoarse** to speak.

2003 – Ram

The **ram's horns** look like a **3 on its side**.

2004 – Monkey

Are **monkeys** our **fore**fathers?

2005 – Rooster

R**005**ter (Remember, 5 looks like the letter S.)

2006 – Dog

2006, **dogs** love **sticks**! (Rhyming link – *sticks* sounds like *six.)*

2007 – Pig

One day, I'm going to be **007**. 'Oh, yeah? **Pigs** might fly!'

2008 – Rat

I **hate rats**. They give me the creeps. (Rhyming link – *hate* sounds like *eight.)*

2009 – Ox

Nine squares in **noughts (O) and crosses (X)**.[1]

2010 – Tiger

A **tiger** is just a big kit**ten**.[1]

2011 – Rabbit

11 looks like a **rabbit's ears**.

[1] These links were created by Claire Adams, West Sussex.

THE 10 BIGGEST
COUNTRIES IN THE WORLD

The total surface area of the Earth is 510,072,000 square kilometres (km²). Of this, 71 per cent is water and only 29 per cent is land! Here are the ten biggest countries of the world in order of their land area, starting with the biggest – Russia!

1. RUSSIA

If you **rush a** lot, you'll probably get there **first**.

Total area: 17,098,242 km²

2. CANADA

a) The **cancan**[1] (two **can**ada)

b) **Two can** play at that game.

(No other country begins with the letters 'Can'.)

Total area: 9,984,670 km²

3. CHINA

'Not by the hair of my **chin**ny-**chin-chin**,' said each of the **three** little pigs.

Total area: 9,572,900 km^2

4. USA

United States of America has **four** words.

Total area: 9,522,055 km^2

5. BRAZIL

Grab a **handful** (**five** digits) of **brazil** nuts.

Total area: 8,514,877 km^2

6. AUSTRALIA

In cricket, **Australia** usually hits every other nation for **six**.

Total area: 7,741,220 km^2

7. INDIA

The Taj Mahal in **India** is one of the **Seven** Wonders of the World.

Total area: 3,287,263 km^2

8. ARGENTINA

Do you know the Simpsons? I love Homer but **hate (eight)** Marge.

Total area: 2,780,400 km^2

9. KAZAKHSTAN

A cat has **nine** lives (**Cat**akhstan).

Total area: 2,724,900 km^2

10. SUDAN

Sudanly we're at number **ten**!

Total area: 2,505,813 km^2

The smallest country of all

The world's smallest country is Vatican City, in Rome, Italy. It's the home of the Pope and has a total area of 0.44 square kilometres, which is about the same size as 60 football pitches. We're talking seriously teeny here, folks!

What makes a country?

Looking at an atlas, you'd have expected Antarctica to be at the top of the list of big countries. But get your head around this: Antarctica is a continent, not a country. What's that all about?

A continent is one of the world's main continuous expanses of land, made up of countries: Europe, Asia, Africa, Australasia, North America, South America, Antarctica. But for a land mass to be a country, it needs to have its own government, and seeing as there are no permanent residents of Antarctica, other than our black-and-white chums with flippers, it can't be a country.

[1] This link was created by Jessica Aitken, East Sussex.

CAPITAL CITIES OF THE WORLD

Around the world in (nearly) 80 stays...

> Try saying these links out loud.
> Some links make more sense if you hear them.

EUROPE

Berlin – Germany
Fast **bowling (Berlin)** does in**jure many** batsmen.

Berne – Switzerland
You'll need to **burn** some calories if you've eaten too much **Swiss** chocolate.

Chisinau – Moldova
a) There's **mould** all **over** the **cheese now**.
b) 'They think it's **Moldova**... it **Chisnau**!' (They think it's **all over**... it **is now**!)[1]

33

Dublin – Eire
Making an **error** can mean **doubling** your workload.

Helsinki – Finland
'Look at that shark! **He'll sink** without his **fin**.'

Madrid – Spain
a) 'This **pain** is driving me **mad. Rid** me of it, please!'
b) 'The rain in **Spain** is driving me **mad. Rid** me of it,
please!'

Oslo – Norway
Fast **or slow**, there's **no way** (**Norway**) you'll complete it.

Paris – France
'My **pa is** competing in the Tour de **France** as he's
wheelie good.'

Reykjavik – Iceland
'Don't **wreck yer fick** milkshake by putting **ice** in it!'

Rome – Italy
It can get b**itterly** cold if you **roam** the streets.

Here's a random phrase for you:

*I just **fell** on my <u>bare</u> **bum** and now it's all <u>black</u>!*

If you look at a map of Europe and read the names of the seven countries on the right-hand side, starting at the top (the <u>Bare</u>nts Sea) and going down to the <u>Black</u> Sea, you'll see that their first letters spell two words: 'fell' and 'bum'.

> **F**inland
> **E**stonia
> **L**atvia
> **L**ithuania
>
> **B**elarus
> **U**kraine
> **M**oldova

These words are known as acronyms. An acronym is a word formed from the initial letters of other words. It's similar to an acrostic (see page 10), but an acronym can be pronounced as a word, whereas an acrostic creates a phrase or sentence.

Latvia and **Lit**huania are handily in alphabetical order.

Brasilia – Brazil
Brazil are **brasilia**nt at football.

Cayenne – French Guiana
What do you get when you cross a **French guy an' a** chess piece? A **KN** (**Knight**).
(KN is the abbreviation for the Knight piece in chess.)

La Paz – Bolivia
'Do another **lap, as** I don't **believe ya.**'

> La Paz is the world's highest capital. 'La Paz' means 'peace'. It must be peaceful being that high up!

Lima – Peru
I love to **peru**se a magazine in the back of my **limou**sine.

Quito – Ecuador
Do mos**quito**es exist in **equator**ial rainforests?

Santiago – Chile
As I'm **Santa, I go** to **Chile** for my holidays.

ASIA

Baghdad – Iraq
'Would you like **a rack** of lamb or a boil-in-the-**bag, Dad**?'

Dhaka – Bangladesh
'Did you **bang the dash**board of **da car** when you braked?'[2]

Doha – Qatar
Do our throats create **catarrh**?

Hanoi – Vietnam
Vietnam war films really **annoy** me.

Islamabad – Pakistan
I slam a bad ball into a **pack**ed **stand**.

Jakarta – Indonesia
My w**indo**w cleaner is **Jack Carter**.

Kuala Lumpur – Malaysia
Is **my lazier (Malaysia) koala a lump or** what?

Manama – Bahrain
a) 'That **brain (Bahrain)** surgeon owns a huge
manor, ma.'
b) **Man, oh ma**n, Einstein had a huge **brain (Bahrain)**.[2]

Muscat – Oman
'**Oh man**, I **must cut** my hair!'

New Delhi – India
Indiana Jones rode a **nude ele**phant.[3]

Apia – Samoa
My gardener is a lot h**appier** if you call him **Sir Mower**.

Canberra – Australia
If you **can burrow** like a mole, you'll end up in **Australia**.

Funafuti – Tuvalu
To value how much **fun a footy** match is, you need to watch a live game.

Wellington – New Zealand
New Zealand is **wellington**-boot-shaped.

NORTH AMERICA

Castries – Saint Lucia
Cash grows on **trees** in **Saint Loot**cia.

George Town – Cayman Islands
'By **George**! This link just **came and** went!'

Hamilton – Bermuda
Lewis **Hamilton** likes to wear **Bermuda** shorts when he drives.

Kingston – Jamaica
D'ya make a king's tongue purple by offering him beetroot?

Nassau – The Bahamas
NASA went **bananas** when Armstrong landed on the Moon.[4]

Oranjestad – Aruba
'Why did you buy me **a rubber orange, Dad**?'

Ottawa – Canada
Can adders eat **otters**?[2]

San Juan – Puerto Rico
'Can **San Juan** tell me **where Terry go**?'

St George's – Grenada

St George's next plan was to throw a **grenad**e at the fire-breathing dragon.

Banjul – Gambia

Do **gamblers** in **Gambia ban jewels** from **Banjul**?[5]

Bamako – Mali

M. Ali … bam! A KO! (Muhammad **Ali … bam! a** knock-**out!** Muhammad Ali was a famous boxer.)

Cairo – Egypt

Mummy's at the **chiro**practor's. (Mummy stands for **Egypt.**)

Dodoma – Tanzania

'How's business at **"Tans in Here"** (**Tanzania**), son?' 'Dead as a **dodo, ma**.'

Gaberone – Botswana
IT **bods wanna (Botswana) gabber on (Gaberone)** about iPod this, Microsoft that…[5]

Khartoum – Sudan
Suddenly the **Cartoon (Khartoum)** Network went offline.

Mogadishu – Somalia
I've bought a new cat. My old **mog had issues** – it was **smellier**.[2]

Rabat – Morocco
Do **Moroccan** ac**robat**s wear fezzes?

Tripoli – Libya
Why spell **Libeeeya** with a **triple 'e' (Tripoli)**?

There are many, many countries out there. Go to www.thinkalink.co.uk and see if you can think of a link for any of their capital cities. Better still, if you can improve on any of the links listed above, then send in your work of magic and let's see what other people think!

42

To cap it all, it's got three capitals!

South Africa doesn't have just one capital city but THREE!

Pretoria is the administrative capital – where the **government** is based.
Cape Town is the legislative capital – where **laws** are passed.
Bloemfontein is the judicial capital – where the **judges** meet in courts.

Here are the links that will help you remember the difference:

Pre**Tory**a: **Tory** is short for the Conservative Party, which runs for **government** in the UK.
Cape Town: Lawbreakers es**cape town**.
Bloem**fontein**: **Judges** need to have a **fountain** of knowledge.

Johannesburg is not one of South Africa's three capital cities, but it is the country's largest city.

[1] This link was created by Mark Kingston, Lincolnshire.

[2] These links were created by Lester Fernando, London.

[3] This link was created by Alan Newell, Berkshire.

[4] This link was created by Claire Adams, West Sussex.

[5] These links were created by Robert Cox, Tyne and Wear.

KINGS and QUEENS of England after 1100

Here are links for the king or queen who was on the throne at the turn of each century from **1100** onwards.

YEAR	KING/QUEEN
1100	*William II (1087–1100)*
	Henry I (1100–1135)

He needs a **Wii** (**Hen** is short for Henry, **W ii** is short for William II and ii looks like **11**).

I can think of six other words that make the Wii sound:

Wee – number one in loo-speak.

We – me and you.

Wee – Scottish for small.

Oui – French for yes.

Weeeeeeeeee! – the noise you make when going down a slide.

Weee! Weee! – the noise a hungry pig makes.

Can you think of any more?

1200   *John (1199–1216)*

a) N**oo**n (**12.00** pm) and J**oh**n have the same second and fourth letters.

1300   *Edward I (1272–1307)*

13 is **E1** backwards.[1]

1400   *Henry IV (1399–1413)*

If you put a digital ⌐ and ⊔ right next to each other they look like an ⊢⊣.

1500   *Henry VII (1485–1509)*

Rugby **15**s and rugby **7**s (**H** are the posts).

1600   *Elizabeth I (1558–1603)*

E**1**iza**6**eth

1700   *William III (1689–1702)*

The **W** and **M** of **WILLIAM** are sideways **3**s and there is an upside-down **17** in the name.

1800 George III (1760–1820)

6eorge x **3** = **18**

1900 Victoria (1837–1901)

Two famous women in England, at the start and the end of the **1900s**, were called **Victoria** (Queen and Beckham).

2000 Elizabeth II (1952–)

2000 – Eli**2**abeth **2**nd

```
Elizabeth  (born  1926)  became  Queen
Elizabeth II on 6 February 1952 and was
          crowned on 2 June 1953.

Her lucky numbers must be two and six -
she became Queen on 6/2 and was crowned
on 2/6. What's more, she was born in '26
      (which is half of '52)!
```

---

[1] This link was created by Jake Tyler, East Sussex.

What a bunch of silly billys! They make me so cross.

The four kings of England called William all had nicknames. The first letters of these nicknames spell CROSS (an acronym!). There are five letters as William IV had two nicknames, both beginning with S:

William I: William the **C**onqueror

William II: William **R**ufus

William III: William of **O**range

William IV: William the **S**ailor King

William IV: **S**illy Billy

William I was Duke of Normandy and the first Norman King of England. He became known as 'the Conqueror' after his conquest of England. To make his claim to the English crown, he invaded England in 1066 at the Battle of Hastings. His victory became known as the Norman Conquest.

William II was called Rufus because he had a red face and 'rufus' means 'red' in Latin.

Now, William III wasn't known as William of Orange because he had been out in the sun too long. It was because he belonged to the royal family of Orange in the Netherlands. The colour orange has now come to symbolize the Netherlands, which is why the national sports teams wear orange.

William IV was nicknamed the 'Sailor King' because he joined the Royal Navy at the very early age of 13. He fell in love with the sea and in 1828 he became the big boss of all the ships, otherwise known as the Lord High Admiral.

William IV was also nicknamed 'Silly Billy' because he never knew when to stop talking, and had a tendency to ramble on for ages and ages. Now 'Silly Billy' is a nickname for any silly or foolish person.

The Twelve Days of Christmas

The Twelve Days of Christmas begin on Christmas Day and end on 5 January, or Twelfth Night – the night before the Three Kings from the East arrived bearing gifts.

The famous carol 'The Twelve Days of Christmas' describes various gifts given on each of the twelve days. The song may have begun as a memory game played on the Twelfth Night many years ago. The players would sing a verse in turn and each player would add a new gift when it came to their own verse – but they had to remember all the previous gifts as they sang their way through the list of presents. Anyone who forgot a gift would have to pay a forfeit to entertain everyone else.

On the first day of Christmas my true love sent to me...

A partridge in a pear tree

A **peartree**dge in a pear tree.

On the second day of Christmas...

Two turtle doves

'Two turtle doves' sounds like 'Two purple gloves'.

On the third day of Christmas...

Three French hens...

...called Ooo, La and La.

On the fourth day of Christmas...

Four calling birds

I'm all **for calling birds** 'our feathered friends'.

On the fifth day of Christmas...

Five gold rings

Five fingers for five gold rings.[1]

On the sixth day of Christmas...

Six geese a-laying

There are six eggs in a box of eggs.

On the seventh day of Christmas...

Seven swans a-swimming

I see **swans swimming** up the River **Severn**.

On the eighth day of Christmas...

Eight maids a-milking

The **milk made** cheese and we **ate** it.[1]

On the ninth day of Christmas...

Nine ladies dancing

Is 'nine dancing' '**line dancing**' for **nine ladies**?

On the tenth day of Christmas...

Ten lords a-leaping

a) Is **Lord** Andrew Lloyd Webber's favourite singer a **ten**or?

b) **Lord**s Cricket Ground? **Ten** out of ten!

On the eleventh day of Christmas...

Eleven pipers piping

The number 11 looks like pipes.

On the twelfth day of Christmas...

Twelve drummers drumming

March to the **drum** beat – **one**, **two**, one, two…

I'm told that at today's prices it would cost about £13,000 to buy all of these gifts!

[1] These links were created by Claire Adams, West Sussex

PHOBIAS

A phobia is an extreme and irrational fear of something. The word comes from the Greek word phobus, which means 'fear'.

There are hundreds and hundreds of phobias, from common ones such as spiders to the craziest things. These everyday heebie-jeebies will make you tremble with fear or sigh 'Oh dear'!

Acrophobia – fear of heights
Acrobats

Agoraphobia – fear of open spaces
'Oi! If you two want to cause some **aggro (agora)**, then go **outside**!'

Algophobia – fear of pain
'**I'll go (algo)** "Ouch!" if it's **pain**ful, doc.'

Altophobia – fear of heights
An **alto** is the **high**est adult male singing voice.

Arachnophobia – fear of spiders
'Are there **spiders** in **Iraq**?'
'**No** idea.'

Claustrophobia – fear of confined spaces
'Blinking **tight spaces**!' grumbled Santa **Claus**, **tra**pped once more in the chimney.

Coulrophobia – fear of clowns
Row Z at the circus is **cool**. **Row** A is too close to those creepy **clowns**!

Ergophobia – fear of work
'You want me to do some **work**? **Er, go** away!'

Gynophobia – fear of women
Yes to a **guy**. **No** to a **woman.**

Hylophobia – fear of forests
Off into the **forest** the seven dwarfs went. '**Hi hoe**, hi hoe, it's off to work we go…'

Melophobia – fear of music
Melody

Ombrophobia – fear of rain
*Ombr*ella
The word umbrella comes from ombrella, which is an Italian word meaning 'little shadow or shade'.

Pantophobia – fear of everything
I hate **everything** about **panto**mimes!

Photophobia – fear of light
I **fear** the flash when they take a **photo** of me.

Polyphobia – *fear of many things*

My pretty **Polly** can say **many things**.

Sitophobia – *fear of food*

'**Sit** over there and I'll bring you your **food**.'

Somniphobia – *fear of sleep*

'**Somebody (somni)** wake me up if I fall **asleep**.'

Xenophobia – *fear of strangers*

Are **there no (xeno)** friendly **strangers** these days?

Where did VERTIGO?

This could well make your head spin. Vertigo is not a fear of heights! In fact, it's not a fear of anything!

It also has nothing to do with the word vertical. Vertigo means either a feeling of whirling and loss of balance or a confused mind.

As with many words in the English language, the names for many phobias are based on Latin or Greek words. For example, 'photophobia' is based on the Greek words phos (meaning 'light') and phobus ('fear'). You now know that somni is linked to 'sleep' (from the Latin somnus, 'sleep') and amble means 'walk', so what do you think 'somnambulist' means? The answer is below.

Answer: sleepwalker

57

ANIMAL SPEEDS IN MILES PER HOUR

Most animals need to cheat a bit to beat a cheetah.

200 mph – peregrine falcon (when in a dive)

In Monopoly, my mate **Perry grins** every time he collects £**200** for passing Go.

100 mph – swift

'Are you **100** per cent sure that's why it's called a **swift**?'

---

70 mph – cheetah

On the motorways, some drivers **cheat a** bit by sneaking over **70 mph**.

---

50 mph – gazelle

Cars don't half (**50** per cent) **guzzle** petrol these days!

50 mph – lion

When sleeping, I **lie on** my back for half (**50** per cent) of the time, then roll on to my side for the other half.

---

45 mph – hare and 40 mph – greyhound

'One, two, three, **four**, **five**, once I caught a **hare** alive…'
'Only because it was grabbing **40** winks at the time, Mr **Greyhound**!'

---

43 mph – shark

In the film *Jaws*, it wasn't looking good **for three** men in a boat…

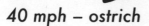

---

40 mph – ostrich

Should I grab **40** winks **or stretch** my legs?

32 mph – reindeer, giraffe

'It's going to **rain, dear**.'
'You're having **a laugh (giraffe)**, aren't you?'
'Feel **free (three) to (two)** leave the brolly behind but…'

30 mph – bear, kangaroo

My dad can't **bear kangaroo**ing over those speed bumps in a **30** mph area.

28 mph – human (running)

Humans hate **to wait** for anything.

MATHS — SQUARED NUMBERS

If you don't remember these links, you'll be back to square one. If a number is squared, it is multiplied by itself. For example, five squared or 5 x 5 = 25. It can be shown by a little two to the top right of the number: 5^2.

---

3 x 3 = 9

In case of emergency, dial **three nine**s.

---

4 x 4 = 16

4.00 pm = **16**:00

---

5 x 5 = 25

5 November versus **25** December? No contest.

---

6 x 6 = 36

I'm **sick (6)**, I'm **sick (6)**, I'm **thirsty (30)** and **sick (6)**.[1]

---

7 x 7 = 49

Heavens (7), **heaven**s (7), I'm **short on time** (49)!

8 x 8 = 64

I **ate** (8) and **ate** (8) until I was **sick** (6) on the **floor** (4).

9 x 9 = 81

'Would you like a **99** ice cream?'
'No thanks, I just **ate** (8) **one**.'

10 x 10 = 100

10 out of **10** is **100** per cent.

11 x 11 = 121

a) **11** is a **1** next **to** (2) a **1**.
b) **11** looks like two people having a **one-to-one** (121).

12 x 12 = 144

One (**1**) **4** x **4** car **doesn't** (dozen = **12**) affect global warming that much.

Here's a neat trick that you can show off to your geeky mates, if you happen to be at a maths convention. It's for working out squared numbers that end in 5: for example, 15 squared, 25 squared, 35 squared, and so on.

Multiply the first digit of the number by itself, +1. Then link the answer with the number 25 (5 x 5) to get the squared total:

35 squared is **3** x (**3** + **1**) = **12**. Linked with **25** (5 x 5) = **1225**.
45 squared is **4** x (**4** + **1**) = **20**. Linked with **25** (5 x 5) = **2025**.
85 squared is **8** x (**8** + **1**) = **72**. Linked with **25** (5 x 5) = **7225**.

[1] This link was created by Phil Newham, Essex.

GRAMMATICAL ERRORS

A grammatical error is the misuse of a word or punctuation mark in a sentence. Once you have learned the meaning and spelling of a word, you need to know how to use the word properly.

Here are some classic slip-ups:

Their (possession) and there (direction)

Their
There[1]

Practice (noun) and practise (verb)

Practice: *Ice* is a noun.
Practise: *Is* is a verb.

Licence (noun) and license (verb)

You need **to see** (**2c**) to obtain a driving li**cenc**e.

Weather *(noun – sun rain, etc) and* *whether* *(conjunction – a doubt or choice between several alternatives)*

The **heat** of the we**at**her.
W**he**ther **he** likes it or not…

Affect (verb) and effect (noun)

RAVEN: Remember, **A**ffect **V**erb, **E**ffect **N**oun

Stationery (noun – writing materials) and stationary (adjective – not moving)

Email is killing off station**e**ry.
A station**ar**y c**ar**.

It's (the short form of 'it is') and *its* (possession)

It's: The apostrophe is a little **i**.

Who's (the short form of 'who is') and *whose* (possession)

Who's: The apostrophe is a little **i**.

Anti (prefix – against or opposed to, eg anti-cars) and ante (prefix – before, in front of in space, eg anteroom = a small room leading into a larger room)

Ant**i** – aga**i**nst
Ant**e** – b**e**for**e**

Principle (noun – ethic/attitude) and *principal* (noun – leader)

Principl**e** – **e**thic
Principa**l** – **l**eader

Compliment (verb – praise) and complement (verb – bring to perfection)

Compliment: 'Save the comp**lime**nts, s**lime**ball!'
Complement: **Comple**te

Compare _with_ (not compare _to_)

Compared w**it**h **it**...

Different _from_ (not different _to_)

The two Fs in _different_ are not di**ff**erent **f**rom each other.

Could _have_ (not could _of_)

If you write 'Could **of**', you'll score a **0** and get an **F** grade.

You're (the short form of 'you are') and your (possession)

Replace the **a** of **a**re with an **a**postrophe.

'My mate and I' or 'Me and my mate'?

Take away 'my mate' and it solves the problem. For example, is it 'my mate and I went to the shops' or 'me and my mate went to the shops'? Leave out the words *my mate*, say the sentence again and you'll quickly work out that it's 'my mate and I'. 'Me went to the shops' just doesn't work!

There should be no apostrophe in 10's 100's 1000's, etc

No apostrophe! (*No* is short for **number**.)

<u>Bear</u> in mind (not <u>bare</u> in mind)

I can't get Paddington **Bear** out of my **mind**!

<u>Hanged</u> or <u>hung</u>?

A m<u>a</u>n is h<u>a</u>nged but a pict<u>u</u>re is h<u>u</u>ng.

HOW LOVELY!

68

Passed (past tense of the verb pass) and past (everything else!)

Pas**sed**: *sed* sounds like *said,* which is a **verb**.

There are many more grammatical blunders out there to think of a link for... But if you start by learning these, you should see a lot more ticks than crosses in your homework books.

*This link was created by Barbara Yandall, Leicestershire.

ANIMAL HOMES

Some animals have more than one name for their home but these are the most commonly used.

Badger – sett

'Stop **badger**ing me and **sett**le down.'

Bat – roost

Are **roost**ers found on **bat**tery farms?

Bear – den

a) Children can be a real **burden** on parents.
b) 'I can't **bear** this! I'm off to my **den** in the garden.'[1]

Beaver – lodge

I'm going to **lodge** at a B&B **for** (beaver) the night.

Fox – earth

What on **earth** is that? It's completely **fox**ed me![1]

Mole – hole

a) 'Holy moly!'[1]
b) '*I am a **mole** and I live in a **hole**.*'[2]

Rabbit – warren

'I'd rather read ***War and Peace*** than listen to you **rabbit** on!'

Squirrel – drey

Squirrel: **D**ull and g**rey** = **drey**.

Lair enough

A lair is a general term for a wild animal's home or resting place.

[1] These links were created by Claire Adams, West Sussex.

[2] This link was created by Alan Newell, Berkshire.

THE MOST POPULATED CITIES OF THE WORLD

Here's a list of the most populated cities in the world as of 2011. Populations change over time, so this might not be the correct order in a few years.

1. Tokyo, Japan

Tokyo Pinocchio (When he lies, his nose looks like the **number one**).[1]

2. Delhi, India

The food at my local **deli** is **too (2)** expensive.

3. São Paolo, Brazil

There are **three footballs** (The letter 'o' looks like a football) in the home of football – **São Paolo**.

4. Mumbai, India

'What did **mum buy for** us?'

5. Mexico City, Mexico

A **Mexican** wave (**Five** digits on a hand).

6. New York, USA

VINYL (**VI** = six in Roman numerals. **NY** = New York. **L** = Loud!)

7. Shanghai, China

I didn't realize how small the **seven** dwarfs were. Never mind knee-high, they're not even **shin-high**!

8. Kolkata, India

Wouldn't you **hate (eight)** to be a **coal cutter**?

9. Dhaka, Bangladesh

'Is **da car** German?'
'**Nein**.' ('No' in German.)

10. Karachi, Pakistan

'You little **tenker, Archie!**'

WOW, THAT'S MEGA!

A megacity is one that has a population of more than ten million people. London (currently 8.3 million) is predicted to hit this figure by 2050.

[1] This link was created by Alexander Salmon, East Sussex.

TIME ZONES (IN HOURS)

In order to measure time, the Earth's surface is divided into 24 wedges, called time zones, that start at Greenwich in London. As you pass over each zone to the east you add 1 hour to the time at Greenwich, and as you pass over each zone to the west you subtract 1 hour.

To remember that the eastern hemisphere is ahead of the western hemisphere, just remember that east is in front of west in the dictionary.

In Britain clocks change twice a year. They move forward by one hour in the spring, and back by one hour in the autumn, which is known as 'fall' in the United States because that's when the leaves fall. This old-timer should help you remember the hour changes...

Spring forward, fall back

The times on the following page show the number of hours a place is behind (-) or ahead (+) of the UK, in the summer months. Some will be an hour or two further ahead or behind in the winter.

-11 Hawaii, USA

Hawa11

-8 Los Angeles (LA), USA

LA + **eight** = L**Ate** (**Ate** sounds like **eight.**)

-6 Mexico

Cor! That **Mexican** chilli has knocked me for **six**!

-6 Chicago, USA

Chicago the Musical hits 'em for **six**!

-5 New York City, USA

Fifth Avenue (a famous street in **New York**).

-4 Rio de Janeiro, Brazil

P**rior** means be**fore**.

+1 _France_

The **Eiffel Tower** looks like a number **1**.

+1 _Spain_

'Have you met my friend **Juan (one)** from **Spain**?'

+1 _South Africa_

One and the SAme (**SA – South Africa**).

+2 _Egypt_

Tutankhamun (a famous **Egyptian** pharaoh).

+3 _Dubai, United Arab Emirates_

Parents **do buy** Duty **Free (three)**.

+3 Moscow, Russia

a) The **Three Moscow**teers
b) 'Brrr! I **must go** (**Moscow**) now – I'm **free**zing!'
(**Free-** sounds like **three**.)

+5 Bangladesh

Bangers on **5** November.

+7 China

The Great Wall of **China** is one of the **Seven** Medieval Wonders of the World.

+7 Singapore

The **Seven** Dwarfs **sing a poor** song but whistle a mean tune – especially while they work!

+8 Tokyo, Japan

I just **ate** a whole **turkey, oh**!

+9 Sydney, Australia

Make sure you're dressed to the **nines** when you go to the **Sydney** Opera House.

+11 Wellington, New Zealand

We**11**ington

'What's the time, me old china?'

China is the third biggest country in the world, and spans the equivalent of five time zones — but the whole country runs on one time. So when it's **11.00** am, and the Sun still hasn't made an appearance in the west of China, have they already been up for a few hours in the dark, or are they still in the Land of Nod? Hmm... my head hurts. I think I need to lie down!

AMERICAN STATES

The United States of America is made up of 50 states. Most people have heard of them all but have problems recalling them. These links will help you to remember how many states begin with a certain letter.

1 state: <u>G</u>eorgia <u>U</u>tah <u>L</u>ouisiana <u>P</u>ennsylvania <u>F</u>lorida <u>D</u>elaware <u>R</u>hode Island <u>H</u>awaii

2 states: <u>S</u>outh Carolina <u>S</u>outh Dakota <u>K</u>ansas <u>K</u>entucky <u>T</u>ennessee <u>T</u>exas <u>V</u>ermont <u>V</u>irginia

3 states: <u>C</u>alifornia <u>C</u>olorado <u>C</u>onnecticut <u>O</u>hio <u>O</u>klahoma <u>O</u>regon

4 states: <u>A</u>labama <u>A</u>laska <u>A</u>rizona <u>A</u>rkansas <u>W</u>ashington <u>W</u>est Virginia <u>W</u>isconsin <u>W</u>yoming <u>I</u>daho <u>I</u>llinois <u>I</u>ndiana <u>I</u>owa

8 states: <u>M</u>aine <u>M</u>aryland <u>M</u>assachusetts <u>M</u>ichigan <u>M</u>innesota <u>M</u>ississippi <u>M</u>issouri <u>M</u>ontana <u>N</u>ebraska <u>N</u>evada <u>N</u>ew Hampshire <u>N</u>ew Jersey <u>N</u>ew Mexico <u>N</u>ew York <u>N</u>orth Carolina <u>N</u>orth Dakota

1 state – G U L P F D R H

Gulp! **FDR** has been taken to hospital (**H**).

(FDR are the initials of Franklin Delano Roosevelt, the US president during the Second World War.)

2 states – S K T V

Are there **too** many channels on **Sk**y **TV**?

3 states – C O

Eco-friendly or **3co**-friendly? [1]

4 states – A W I

I'd like **a Wi**i **for** Christmas.

8 states – M N

Wisdom does **emanate** (**MN8**) from this link.

A quick quiz question for you. Fingers on buzzers...

In which states would you find the most northerly, southerly, westerly and easterly points of the USA?

Clue: Three of the answers are the same state!

Answers:

Northerly – Alaska
Southerly – Hawaii
Westerly – Alaska
Easterly – Alaska

In the word *Alaska*, 'A' is the most **westerly** and **easterly** letter. 'A' is also the most **northerly** letter in the alphabet. The island of Hawaii is found in the **South** Pacific.

Alaska is an enormous American state found between Canada and Russia on the west coast. Here, there are only 50 miles between Russia and the United States. The body of water called the Bering Strait separates the two countries.

Here's a link for remembering the location of the Bering Strait:

The **East** (Russia) is **bearing** down on the **West** (America).

In 1867 the Americans bought Alaska off the Russians for $7.2 million.

The Rat Islands, which are part of Alaska, lie very close to the 180° line of longitude that separates the eastern and western hemispheres. This is the most easterly place in the US.

An explorer named the Rat Islands after the rats he saw scurrying all over them. But now there are no rats left on the Rat Islands, so maybe they should just be called the Islands!

[1] This link was created by Claire Adams, West Sussex.

STATE CAPITALS OF AMERICA

You now know the 50 states of America, so how about trying to remember their capital cities? Here are some links for a selection of them...

Alaska – Juneau

'D'you know (**Juneau**) where we are?'
'No, but she might, **I'll ask her**.'[1]

Arizona – Phoenix

If he nicks (**Phoenix**) the lead from **Harry's owner** (**Arizona**), Harry will have to be carried home!

Arkansas (pronounced Ark-an-saw!) – Little Rock

'I threw a **little rock** at Noah's **Ark and saw** it sink.'

Hawaii – Honolulu

'Excuse me, where should my daughter do **her wee-wee**?'
'**On a loo loo**, madam!'

Idaho – Boise

'Oh, **I dunno, boys**. Ask your dad.'

Illinois – Springfield

Springfield's Homer**'ll annoy** you very little – he's hilarious!

Kansas – Topeka

I wonder if anyone **can suss** how to make a **2p car**?

Kentucky – Frankfort

I much prefer a **Kentucky** Fried Chicken to a **Frankfurt**er.

Maine – Augusta

The birth sign Leo (a lion) is **mane**ly in **August**. [2]

Missouri – Jefferson City

'Stop being a **misery**! I won't be a **jiffy, son**.'

Montana – Helena

Is **Helena Montana** Hannah's twin sister?

New Jersey – Trenton

My **new jersey** makes me look like I've got a **tent on**!

Ohio – Columbus

'Christopher **Columbus** never stops travelling …
Oh, hi … oh, he's gone, again!'

Tennessee – Nashville

a) Dennis the **Mennessee** and **Gnasherville**.[2]
b) Smashville, Tennissee

Texas – Austin

A marathon **takes us** (**Texas**) so long to run, it's exh**austin**'.[2]

87

Washington – Olympia

This **washing** weighs a **ton** – that's why **I limp here (Olympia)**.[3]

Can you think of a link for any of the other American states and their capitals? If so, send it to:

www.thinkalink.co.uk

Remember, you don't need to link every syllable of each word. Just the main bits.

RIDICULOUS FACT:
Montpelier in Vermont is the only state capital without a McDonald's.

No M(cDonald's) is in both words backwards – **Mont**pelier and Ver**mon**t.

[1] This link was created by Sarah Kaufmann, USA.

[2] These links were created by Phil Stubbs, Derbyshire,

[3] This link was created by Phil Isaac, Cornwall.

CAT'S EYES – Percy Shaw

Purrcy Shaw lit up the world with this invention!

CRISPS – George Crum

Crumbs, it's burned to a **crisp**! A **gorge**ous meal ruined. [1]

ELECTRIC MOTOR – Michael Faraday

How **far a day** can you go in that **electric**-powered **motor**?

ICE CREAM – Jacob Fussell

What's the **fuss all** about with these new **Jacob**'s **ice-cream** crackers?

INTERNET – Tim Berners-Lee

Does a tree **timber nicely inter** the **net**?

JET ENGINE – Frank Whittle

To be **frank**, a **jet engine** should be jet black instead of **white all** over.

LIGHT BULB – Thomas Edison

A **light bulb** in Thomas's **head is on** (**Edison**).

PENICILLIN – Alexander Fleming

'Do I take **penicillin** for this **phlegm in** (**Fleming**) my throat, doc?'

PLANE – Wilbur and Orville Wright

The plane will burn up **or will** fly. Let's see who's **right**.

SAFETY MATCH – Gustaf Pasch

My dog Patch invented the **safety match** – **good stuff, Patch**!

STETHOSCOPE – René Laennec

A **stethoscope** hangs around **la neck** of a French doctor.

TELEVISION – John Logie Baird

The TV cartoon character **Yogi Bear** sounds like **Logie Baird**.

WIND-UP RADIO – *Trevor Baylis*

'**Trevor Baylis** on the "Clever A-list"?'[1]
'Yeah, it was on the **radio** so it may be a **wind-up**!'[2]

The scientist Thomas Edison (1847–1931) is considered to be one of the most prolific inventors ever. He created many devices that had a huge impact on the world, including the record player, motion picture camera and the electric light bulb.

[1] This link was created by Claire Adams, West Sussex.

[2] This link was created by James Paterson, Berkshire.

BONES OF THE BODY

Skull – cranium

B**rainium** cranium

Jaw – mandible

'**Man! The bill** is **jaw**-dropping, waiter!'

Collar bone – clavicle

This is one **clever, cool** customer who never gets hot under the **collar**.

Shoulder – scapula

Dracula and his Scapula? We'll be giving that film the cold **shoulder**.

Lower arm (inner and outer bones) – radius and ulna

I'll know (ulna) how big the **radius** of Popeye's arms can get when he's eaten some spinach.

Wrist – carpal

'Hey, what's my **wrist**watch doing in your **car, pal**?'

Hand – metacarpal

I **met a couple** and offered them my **hand**.

Chest – sternum

Finding a treasure **chest** is a **stern** test.

Back – vertebrae

'Does father pre**fer to pray** farther **back** in the church?'

Hip bones – pelvis

Elvis swivels his **hips**.[1]

Knee – patella

'Mum's so embarrassing. **Pa, tell her** to get off your **knee**!'

Calf – fibula

'Cor! You don't h**alf fib**!'

Shin – tibia

To be a footballer, you need **shin** pads.

Upper arm (ending at the elbow) – humerus

My **funny bone** is at the end of my **humorous**.[2]

Ankle – tarsal

Sand**castle**s are usually **ankle**-high.

Foot – metatarsal

a) I've just bought some **footwear** with **metal tassel**s.
b) We **met at Ars**enal **Foot**ball Club.

'Mum, where have my BONES gone?'

Did you know that a newborn baby has more than 300 bones but an adult has only 206? That's because, during growth, lots of the smaller bones fuse together to make bigger ones. Here's a link to help you remember that an adult human's body has 206 bones:

**Bones** sounds like _**bonez**_, which contains the number _**206**_ backwards – _**60ne2**_.

[1] This link was created by Tom Chivers, East Sussex.

This link was created by Sarah Kaufmann, USA.

GREEK GODS AND GODDESSES

In Ancient Greek mythology the 12 great gods and goddesses were known as the Olympians. They lived at the top of Mount Olympus, from which they got their name.

The Greeks and Romans used the same system of gods but gave them different names. These are some of the most famous. The links for the Greek gods contain references to Greece, so you won't mix them up with their Roman cousins.

King of the Gods – Zeus

<u>Greek</u> *Eggs and Ham* by **King Zeus**.

God of love – Eros

I **love** <u>Olympic</u> he**ro**es.

Goddess of the Harvest and Grains (Cereal) – Demeter

'What's **de matter**?'
'Someone's put <u>Greek</u> yoghurt on my **cereal**.'

God of Light – Apollo (the same for both Greek and Roman names)

A Polo is a very **light** car to drive.

Goddess of the Sea – Poseidon

Poseides (**besides**) <u>greasy</u> oil slicks, swimming in the **sea** is great.

God of War – Ares

Computer soft**ware's** all <u>Greek</u> to me!

God of Wine – Dionysus

'Poisoned <u>Greek</u> **wine** means he could **die on us**!'[1]

Goddess of Wisdom – Athena

It's **wise** to eat Greek yoghurt if you want **a thinner** body.

ROMAN GODS AND GODDESSES

In Ancient Rome the 12 great gods and goddesses were known as the Dii Consentes.

These links contain references to Rome or Italy (Rome is the capital of Italy), so you won't mix the Roman gods up with the Greek ones.

King of the Gods – Jupiter

In terms of size, Jup<u>it</u>er is **king** of the planets.
(<u>It</u> is short for Italy.)

Queen of the Gods – Juno

'**D'you know** what the **Queen**'s favourite <u>pasta</u> is?'

God of Fire – Vulcan

Volcanic fire of erupting <u>Vesuvius</u>.
(The word volcano comes from Vulcan, and Vesuvius is a volcano in Italy.)

Goddess of Harvest and Grains (cereal) – Ceres

Do fit people eat **cere**al?
(The word 'cereal' comes from Ceres.)

God of Light – Apollo (the same for both Greek and Roman names)

You can shine a **light** through **a Polo** mint.[1]

Goddess of Love – Venus

Venus Williams to serve at the <u>Italian</u> Open…
15-**Love**.

Goddess of the Moon and Hunting – Diana

If the <u>Mafia</u> are **hunting** you, there's every chance
you'd **die in a** nasty way.

God of the Sea – Neptune

When you **tune** a <u>piano</u>, you start with Middle **C**.
(Piano is an Italian word.)

God of Travellers and Messengers – Mercury

Mercury has the shortest orb<u>it</u>, so it **travels** around the Sun the quickest.

God of Love – Cupid

I'm just a st**upid** <u>romantic</u> who can't help falling in **love**.

God of the Underworld – Pluto

Pluto chases **sticks** in the streets of <u>Rome</u> (**Styx** – the river of the **underworld**).

[1] These links were created by Phil Isaac, Cornwall.

THE SIX WIVES OF HENRY VIII

King Henry VIII is famous for his six wives and his cruel behaviour towards them. Here's a catchy old rhyme for remembering the fate of each wife:

DIVORCED, BEHEADED, DIED;
DIVORCED, BEHEADED, SURVIVED

And here are some links to help you recall the wives' names in chronological order:

1. Catherine of Aragon
Arrogant people look after number **one**.

2. Anne Boleyn
You have **two** goes in ten pin **bowlin**g.[1]

3. Jane Seymour
If only the **three** blind mice could **see more**…[1]

4. Anne of Cleves
Four-cleve clover.

5. Catherine Howard
Handy Howard (a handful is **five**).

6. Catherine Parr
A **cat** has a **sixth** sense? **Pah**![1]

If you want to remember which two wives had their heads chopped off, this might help:

The first letters of the first two syllables of '**beh**eaded' are **B** for **Boleyn** and **H** for **Howard**.

And here's another way to remember all the wives in order:

Aragon
Boleyn
Seymour
Cleves
Howard
Parr

A.B's for the **CHOP!**

In all, the nasty King Henry VIII executed 72,000 people. I can name two of them. Can you name the other 71,998?

[1] These links were created by Claire Adams, West Sussex.

Historical Dates

871 – Alfred the Great became King

Did Alfred the Gr**8** ever see any of the **Seven Won**ders of the World?

1066 – The Battle of Hastings

Clickety click, hit with a stick, the **Battle of Hastings** was in **1066**.[1]

1215 – Magna Carta (a legal agreement that King John was forced to sign, limiting his power)

King John was a bit of a goon.
He signed the **Magna Carta** at a **quarter past noon (12.15)**.[2]

1300s – Black Death (in Europe)

If you link the numbers **1** and **3**, you get **B** for **Black**.

1588 – Spanish Armada

I **won (1)** a **5**-star meal and **ate (8)** and **ate (8)** till I was in **pain (Spain)**. But I was fine because **I'm 'arder (Armada)** than you think.[3]

1605 – The Gunpowder Plot

There was a **BANG** at the door at **five past four (16.05)**.

1642–51 – English Civil War

At **16.00** hours the civil English traditionally have tea **for two**, holding the cup with **five** fingers, **one** sticking out.[3]

1666 – Great Fire of London

666 is said to be the number of the Devil and his **fires** of hell.

1775 – The American War of Independence

I'm **17** and **three quarters (75%)** … **independence** is just around the corner.

1805 – Battle of Trafalgar

De sweet sank (dix-huit cinq) to the bottom of the fountain in **Trafalgar** Square.
(In French, dix-huit is 18 and cinq is five.)

1815 – Battle of Waterloo

At **eighteen and a quarter** hours (**18.15**)
Boney fell to allied powers.
Prussians, French and British too
Had a fight at **Waterloo**.[4]

1912 – the Titanic went down...

...even though the engines were going **nineteen** to the **dozen** (a dozen is 12).

1914–18 – First World War

People **fought in** (14) and **ate in** (18) awful conditions and were always **thirst**y (**first**).

1939–45 – Second World War

In '39 Poland was fine. In '45 was Hitler alive? [5]

1952 – Queen Elizabeth II came to the throne

Every year (**52** weeks) the **Queen** gives her Christmas speech.

1953 – Edmund Hillary was the first to climb Mount Everest

Some joker (**53rd** card in the pack) claims to have climbed **Mount Everest**. **He really** (**Hillary**) must be having a laugh.

1969 – Neil Armstrong walked on the Moon, and said…

'One small step for a man. One giant leap for mankind.' The speech marks look like a **6** and a **9**.

There are loads more dates and events that you could link. Why not think of a link and send it to:

www.thinkalink.co.uk

[1] This link was created by Mike Campbell, West Sussex.

[2] This link was created by Phil Moore, Wiltshire.

[3] These links were created by Claire Adams, West Sussex.

[4] This link was created by Phil Isaac, Cornwall.

[5] This link was created by Michael Shaladay, London.

How to Convert Degrees Celsius to Degrees Fahrenheit

To convert degrees Celsius (°C) to degrees Fahrenheit (°F), you need to multiply the Celsius total by 1.8, then add 32. But that's far too complicated, so try these links as a guideline.

0°C = 32°F

a) In tennis, **3-2** in sets meant there was nothing **(0)** in it.
b) **No (0)** months have **32** days.

Water freezes at 0°C/32°F.

5°C = 41°F

'Let's take **five for one** moment…'

16°C = 61°F

1661 is symmetrical.

19°C = 66°F

England won the Football World Cup in **1966**.

25°C = 77°F

The Queen's Silver Jubilee (**25** years) was in 1977.

28°C = 82°F

2882 is symmetrical.

38°C = 100°F

Arsenal are the only team to have a **100** per cent unbeaten record in a Premiership season (**38** games).

40°C = 104°F

40104 is symmetrical.

50°C = 122°F

In **5**-a-side football (**0**), it's a **1-2-2** formation.

Of course, there are many more numbers between 0 and 50 that need to be linked. Here are a few that I seem to be making heavy weather of. See if you can think of a link before my blood boils over...

7 °C = 45°F   15°C = 59°F   20°C = 68°F
21°C = 70°F   32°C = 90°F   35°C = 95°F

We're talking extreme weather, folks!

Hottest place on Earth: El Azizia, Libya, 57.8 °C/136 °F (recorded 13 September 1922)

LINK: **Hell has easier (El Azizia)** ways of giving you a top-up tan than this **oven**!

Coldest place on Earth: Antarctic, -89.4 °C/ -129 °F (recorded 21 July 1983)

LINK: There was a **cold** atmosphere when **Ant** told Dec that he was leaving.

Driest place on Earth: Atacama Desert, Chile (some parts haven't seen rain for more than 400 years!)

LINK: You'll never be **at a calmer** place on earth. As **deserts** go, it's surprisingly **chilly**!

Wettest pace on Earth (unofficial world record): Cherrapunji, India (once, it didn't stop raining for two years!)

LINK: We **cheer a bungee**-jumper when their head goes in the **water**.

Cherrapunji gets so much rain (an average of 13 metres per year) because it's so high above sea level. However, it still suffers from severe water shortages – so many trees have been cut down that the soil can't absorb water very well. The water runs down to Bangladesh, which really doesn't need the extra water as it's also an extremely wet part of the world!

Maths — Cubed Numbers

Cubed numbers are formed by multiplying a digit by itself three times. For example:

4 cubed is 4 x 4 x 4 = 64

2 cubed is 8

You have **to wait (2 8)** in a queue.

3 cubed is 27

Three steps **to heaven (2 7)**.

4 cubed is 64

The Beatles (The Fab **Four**) sang 'When I'm **64**'.

5 cubed is 125

From **one to five (1 2 5)**, **five** is the biggest.

6 cubed is 216

From **six to 16 (6216)**, there are **six** even numbers.

7 cubed is 343

'How did Man United do in the last **seven** days?'
'They won all three games – so they were **three for three (343)**.'

8 cubed is 512

a) **Five**, **one** and **two** are 'pieces of **eight**'.
b) 'I **hate (8)** to lose a tennis match, especially if **I've won two (5 1 2)** sets,' whinges Murray.[1]

9 cubed is 729

a) 'Help, police **(999)**! The **Seven** Dwarfs are trying **to mine (2 9)** some diamonds illegally!'[2]
b) In the evening, Big Ben chimes **9** times from **7 to 9** (every quarter of an hour).

How to tell if a number can be divided by 3

Add the digits in the number up. If the total can be divided by 3, then so can the number itself. For example, take the five-figure number 26,745: $2 + 6 + 7 + 4 + 5 = 24$. The total 24 can be divided by 3, which means 26,745 can also be divided by 3!

[1] This link was created by Alan Newell, Berkshire.

[2] This link was created by Shane Fernando, Spain.

3 x 4 = 12

12 = 3 x 4   (**1 2 3 4**)

3 x 6 = 18

She licks a **plate clean**, **3 6**s are **18**.[1]

3 x 7 = 21

a) **Bee heaven** is **plenty** of **sun**, **3 7**s are **21**.[1]
b) The **key** to **heaven** is **plenty** of **fun**, **3 x 7** is **21**.

3 x 8 (or 8 x 3) = 24

a) I **ate (8) 3** meals in **24** hours.[2]
b) **8** hours of work, **8** hours of rest and **8** hours of play make up my **24**-hour day.

4×6 (or 6×4) = 24

I hit a **6** and a **4**, I'll score **plenty more**. $6 \times 4 = 24$.

$4 \times 7 = 28$

There are **4** weeks (**7** days) in the **28** days of February.

$4 \times 8 = 32$

My **poor mate**'s got **birdie flu**, **4** **8**s are **32**.[1]

$6 \times 7 = 42$

I play **tricks** on **Kevin** but he's **naughty too**, $6 \times 7 = 42$.

$6 \times 8 = 48$

My **sick mate**'s **naughty** and **late**, **6** **8**s are **48**.[1]

$7 \times 8 = 56$

$56 = 7 \times 8$ (5 6 7 8)

How to calculate multiples

A multiple of a number is what you get when you multiply that number by some other whole number – eg $3 \times 5 = 15$, so 15 is a multiple of 3.

MULTIPLES OF 5
a) Halve the number then multiply by 10.
eg $4 \div 2 = 2 \times 10 = 20$. ($20 = 4 \times 5$)
b) Think of a clock face, as the numbers are spaced out every 5 minutes. For example, if you know that the number 8 on a clock is 40 minutes past, then you'll know that $5 \times 8 = 40$. The number 4 is 20 minutes past, so $5 \times 4 = 20$.[3]

MULTIPLES OF 9 (UP TO 10)
a) Hold both your hands out, and number your fingers 1-10, from the little finger on your left hand to the little finger on your right hand. Hold down the finger which corresponds to the number you want to multiply by nine. So if you want to work out 3×9, hold down your third finger. Look at the fingers that are left sticking up. You'll have a two and a seven – 27!

b) Here is the 9 times table:
$2 \times 9 = 18$, $3 \times 9 = 27$, $4 \times 9 = 36$,
$5 \times 9 = 45$, $6 \times 9 = 54$, $7 \times 9 = 63$,
$8 \times 9 = 72$, $9 \times 9 = 81$, $10 \times 9 = 90$.

There are two things to notice about this sequence:

• The first digit of the multiple is always one less than the number you are multiplying 9 by: for example, $\underline{2}$ and $\underline{1}8$, $\underline{4}$ and $\underline{3}6$.

• The two digits in the multiple always add up to nine: for example, 36 (3 + 6 = 9), 72 (7 + 2 = 9).

MULTIPLES OF 10
Simply add a zero!

MULTIPLES OF 11 (SINGLE-DIGIT NUMBERS)
As 1 is written down twice to get 11, write the number down twice to get the answer. For example, 11 x 6 = 66.

MULTIPLES OF 11 (DOUBLE-DIGIT NUMBERS)
Add the digits together and place the total between them. (If the total is 10 or greater, then carry the one.) For example, 11 x 24 is '2 (2 + 4) 4' = 264.

MULTIPLES OF 12
Multiply by 10 (add a zero), then add that to the original number, doubled. For example, 12 x 6 = 60 + 12 (6 x 2) = 7.

[1] These links were created by Phil Newham, Essex.

[2] This link was created by Keeley Hanson, London.

[3] This link was created by Lulu Salmon, East Sussex.

MEANINGS OF WORDS

Linking works for any fact, and that includes knowing what a word means, whether it be English, French, Spanish or alienspeak!

Wouldn't it be nifty to be able to tell someone you know the meaning of every word of this English language malarkey – and we're talking the whole shebang? Not only would it bamboozle people but it would freak them out, leaving them flabbergasted. They would probably say 'Codswallop!' and call you a nincompoop.

We know where virtually every word comes from. However, there are some that we just don't have the first clue about. That's what makes our language fun. This crazy gang are of unknown origin:

BAMBOOZLE bonkers CODSWALLOP
flabbergast FREAK higgledy-piggledy
LUMMOX malarkey NIFTY nincompoop
NITTY-GRITTY pernickety RINKY-
DINK scallywag SCOUNDREL shenanigan
SHEBANG skedaddle SNITCH swizzle

You can pick your own favourite but mine, by a country mile, is bonkers. It just sounds so right and doesn't need an explanation.

The average six-year-old has a 10,000-word vocabulary. It is estimated that more than 100,000 different words are in books and other reading materials used by children throughout their school years. Having to learn the meaning of all these words is a time-consuming process and, to be frank, a tad dull.

But worry not.
Don't lose the plot.
Check out Sir Linkalot
And see what he's got.

SIR LINKALOT'S HEALTH WARNING

Before we go any further in this section, prepare yourself for lots of cheesy puns. Playing around with words to discover their meaning is not only a giggle but a challenge I relish (and I'm not talking about something to accompany my burger here).

Let's begin, appropriately, with the word homophone —
a word that sounds like another but has a different meaning.
For example, flower and flour.

Puns and homophones are closely connected. So it would be
nice to use the linking technique of word play to remember
the meaning of this splendid word.

Here are two links, because a homophone has two meanings:

HOMOPHONE: what a homing pigeon uses if it's lost.

HOMOPHONE: the phone at the Simpson's residence.

You hear the following expressions in everyday life:

Lions roar Bees buzz Sheep baa
Babies bawl Birds cheep Doors slam

These verbs have a special name that is worth learning
because, first, it would be very useful to know and, second, it
is one of the silliest words you are likely to bump into:

Onomatopoeia: a word that imitates the sound of the word it describes.

Close your eyes and say these six syllables of madness over and over again... on-o-mat-o-pee-a.

I opened the front door and **on a mat a pair** of lions were lying there **roaring** like a couple of good'uns.

'Roar' is a good example of onomatopoeia – when you say it, it sounds like a deep and scary noise.

Sounds familiar

A strong link is when the word you are trying to remember already sounds like something else. So no vowel or consonant tweaking is required.

Surreal: something resembling a dream or unrealistic

I've just been crowned **Sir Reel**, World Fishing Champion. I must be **dream**ing.

FELON: a person who has committed a serious crime

Was it a **serious crime** if a huge man **fell on** a little lady?

INNATE: natural

Could a **natural** sprinter run the 100 metres **in eight** seconds flat?

YOU MAKE ME LAUGH, YOU DO!

You can have so much fun altering the sound of a word that incy-wincy bit.

Knights, like my good self, are known for their chivalry. So...

CHIVALRY: gentlemanly behaviour

Shiver me (chivalry) timbers! A gentlemanly pirate!

STEED: a horse

'Whoa there! **Stead**y now, **stead**y…'

SURLY: bad-tempered

It'**s early** in the morning, I'm bound to be **bad-tempered**!

INFER: to deduce

I'm **in for** it now. I've just spilt **de juice** all over the floor.

SURFEIT: an excessive amount (especially food and drink)

'Will **slr fit** into his trousers having **eaten too much**?'[1]

DISCOURSE: a conversation

Discourse sounds like *discuss*.

Sometimes all that's required is to change a letter or two:

SULLEN: *sulky or grumpy*

Sulken

FOLLY: *a foolish action or idea*

Fooly

HIRSUTE: *hairy or untrimmed*

A **hair suit**

HOLISTIC: *concerned with the whole rather than parts*

Wholeistic

CULPABLE: *guilty or deserving of blame*

a) Gulpable
b) A **culp**rit is normally **culp**able. (The word *culprit* comes from *culpable*.)

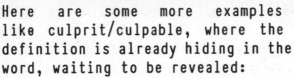

Here are some more examples like culprit/culpable, where the definition is already hiding in the word, waiting to be revealed:

COVERT: *concealed or secret*

Covert

PURGE: *to cleanse or make pure*

a) **Purge**
b) I have the **urge** to **P**.[2]

Combative: *inclined to fight/aggressive*

Combative

Linking something to famous people or characters is always a popular move:

WIZENED: *shrivelled or wrinkled (especially with age)*

The **Wizened** of Oz ended up being a wrinkled old man.

APPEASE: *to calm or soothe*

Was Mr **Happy's** mission to **calm** Mr Jelly?

MISDEMEANOUR: *misbehaviour or a minor offence*

Mr Mean or not, being so ungenerous is an **offence.**

DRACONIAN: *extremely harsh or severe (like teachers can be!)*

Dracula can be a **severe** pain in the neck.

Let's finish off this 'word definition' section with an assortment of words using various linking techniques:

HIDE (NOUN): skin

Hide your **skin** when you're out in the sun.

AVID: very keen or enthusiastic

A vid's OK but I'm really **keen** on watching a DVD.

BRACE (NUMBER): two

A pair of braces.

EXHUME: to remove from a grave

Grave robbers **exhume** an **ex-hum**an.

TORQUE: a turning or twisting force

'I'll **twist** your arm until you **talk**!'

DOTAGE: feeble-mindedness through old age

Dotty **age**.

RECALCITRANT: *a willfully disobedient or stubborn person*

'**Wreck all**! **Sit**! **Rant**!' (Try saying this one out loud – it should help!)

PENITENT: *feeling or showing sorrow or regret*

You need to **bow your head** to enter a one-**penny tent**.

LASSITUDE: *weariness or lack of energy*

Lassie chewed on her bone so much that she grew **weary**.

PROFFER: *to propose or offer*

Propose **offer**

REPAST: *a meal*

He passed it, then **re-passed** it, making a real **meal** out of finding the place.

AUSTERE: stern or severe

You can drive a boat from the bow, **or steer** it from the **stern**.

SUBSERVIENT: eager to carry out someone's wishes; of less importance or rank

'Serv' 'ent' sounds like 'servant'.

VERTIGINOUS: whirling or dizziness

Vertigo makes everything **spin** round and round...

SEVER: to cut off, divide or separate

'Gosh, that's a **sever**e hair**cut**!'

GREGARIOUS: Fond of company or sociable

Meeting places for people called Greg (**Greg areas**).

---

[1] This link was created by Mark Williams, West Sussex.

[2] This link was created by Bridget Ryland, London.

ROMAN NUMERALS

The Ancient Romans used a number system made up of seven letters: **I V X L C D M**. Roman numerals are still seen on clocks and watches today.

1 = I
I looks like 1.[1]

5 = V
Fi**V**e[2]

10 = X
E**X**tend[2]

40 = XL
A pop group needs to **excel** (XL) to get a song into the Top **40**.

50 = L
50 Roman **50L**diers.

100 = C
A **C**entury is **100** years.

500 = D
500 AD – the start of the **DA** (**D**ark **A**ges).

1000 = M
A **M**illennium is **1000** years.

What's the score with this I, V and X stuff then?

There are various theories as to the origin of these Roman numerals but the following explanation seems to be the most accepted:

A tally stick was an ancient memory-aid device to record numbers, quantities or even messages. 'I' comes from a notch

133

scored across a tally stick. Every fifth notch was a double cut (V) and every tenth was a cross cut (X). Every tenth V had an extra notch above it, which after a while took the shape of an L. C stands for century, D stands for demi-mille (half-thousand) and M stands for mille (thousand).

---

[1] This link was created by Claire Adams, West Sussex.

[2] These links were created by Alan Newell, Berkshire.

THE PERIODIC TABLE

The Periodic Table shows the chemical elements ordered by their atomic number. Scientists are discovering elements all the time but there are currently **118**, and **94** of these are found naturally on Earth. The others are too unstable to be found on Earth and are called 'synthetic elements'.

All the different elements are arranged in a chart called:

THE PERIODIC TABLE.

* The horizontal rows are called periods.
* The vertical columns are called groups.

Each element has a symbol (usually one or two letters, shown in brackets after the name of the element)...

The only letter that doesn't appear in the Periodic Table is J.

SIR LINKALOT'S TIP

You only need to link the first syllable if no other element begins with the same sound.

1. Hydrogen (H)

a) 'Hi everyone.'
b) Hydrogen is the highest element. Hence number one.

2. Helium (He)

a) Two heels.[1]
b) Helium balloons take you to (2) a higher place.[2]

3. Lithium (Li)

a) Lithreeum[3]
b) Three Little Pigs

4. Beryllium (Be)

a) Vote for Beryl!
b) A bear has four legs.
c) A bare forehead.

5. Boron (B)

a) Does school bore on all five days of the week?
b) It's never a bore on 5 November.

6. Carbon (C)

Feeling **car sick's** (**6**) horrible.

7. Nitrogen (N)

Seven nights of the week.

8. Oxygen (O)

Oxygen sounds like **octagon**, an **eight**-sided shape.

9. Fluorine (F)

Fluorince **Nine**tingale

10. Neon (Ne)

a) In **ten**-pin bowling, you put your **knee on** the floor.
b) **10 neon** bottles standing on the wall…

11. Sodium (Na)

This element is **so dumb**, it can't add up **one** and **one**!

12. Magnesium (Mg)

Doesn't (dozen) magnesium help to keep teeth strong?

13. Aluminium (Al)

It's **unlucky (13)** to walk under an **aluminium** ladder.

14. Silicon (Si)

Valentine's Day (14 February) is just a **silly con**.

15. Phosphorus (P)

'Don't make a **fuss for us 15**,' insisted the rugby team.

16. Sulphur (S)

In chess the **16** pawns **suffer (sulphur)** more than the other pieces.

17. Chlorine (Cl)

In a **chlorine**-infested Olympic swimming pool, there is **one** winner and **seven** losers.

18. Argon (Ar)

Your childhood years **are gone** when you turn **18**.[2]

19. Potassium (K)

England hit the jack**pot** in **19**66 winning the Football World Cup.

20. Calcium (Ca)

Drink milk for **calcium**, not J**20**.[1]

As a back-up, here's an easy way to remember the elements 13 to 19:

'My teenage mate Alan "Al" Clark is always taking a sip of everyone's drinks. It's really annoying. So we've nicknamed him **Al "Sips" Clark**.'

This spells out the symbols of the elements from 13 to 19 (teenage years): **Al, Si, P, S, Cl, Ar, K**.

Aluminium (**Al**)   Silicon (**Si**)   Phosphorus (**P**)
Sulphur (**S**) Chlorine (**Cl**) Argon (**Ar**) Potassium (**K**)

Here's a selection of other elements, with many more waiting to be linked at www.thinkalink.co.uk.

26. Iron (Fe)

a) The **Iron** Man triathlon includes a **26**-mile marathon.
b) You need **iron** lungs to run a **26**-mile marathon.
Heavy (F E) going or what?

29. Copper (Cu)

'If the lollipop lady isn't there by quarter **to nine (2 9)**, the **copper** will **see you (C U)** you across the road.'

47. Silver (Ag)

It's a race to b**ag** the **silver for (4)** the **seven (7)** running against Usain Bolt.

50. Tin (Sn)

Tin is **50** per cent of **Tin**tin, whereas **Sn** is not 50 per cent of Snowy.

79. Gold (Au)

a) In *Star Trek: Voyager* does **Seven** of **Nine** have **gold**en or **au**burn hair?[3]

b) My d**au**ghter eats **Gold**en Nuggets between **seven** and **nine**.

82. Lead (Pb)

Having **lead** for most of the race, wouldn't you **hate to (8 2)** lose, especially if you ran a personal best (**PB**)?

---

[1] These links were created by Claire Adams, West Sussex.

[2] These links were created by Alan Newell, Berkshire.

[3] These links were created by Phil Isaac, Cornwall.

BIRTHSTONES

A birthstone is a precious stone that symbolizes the month of birth. Some months have more than one gemstone, but these tend to be the most popular.

January – garnet
Darn it! January already?[1]

February – amethyst
Is **St Valentine a myth**?

March – aquamarine
Aqua**mar**ine

April – diamond
Buying me a **diamond** ring is **a brill** idea.

May – emerald
May Queen **Emma ruled** for a day.

June – pearl
A **pearl** washed up on a sand **dune**.[2]

July – ruby
Judy (**July**) Garland wore **ruby** slippers.[3]

August – peridot
It's **peri dot (very hot)** in **August**.

September – sapphire
I **slept** on the **sofa (sapphire)**.

October – opal
In **October**, I always give trick-or-treaters **Opal** Fruits.

November – topaz
I like **to pass (topaz)** the time of day by reading a **nov**el.

December – turquoise
December is the month for **turkeys (turquoise)**.

[1] This link was created by Sarah Kaufmann, USA.

[2] This link was created by Claire Adams, West Sussex.

[3] This link was created by Phil Isaac, Cornwall.

THE SEVEN WONDERS OF THE ANCIENT WORLD

The Seven Wonders of the Ancient World is a list of the seven most impressive ancient monuments in the Mediterranean and Middle Eastern regions. Many similar lists have been made, including lists for the medieval world and the modern world.

LINK: The first letters of the locations spell 'A GB HERO' (a Great Britain hero in the Olympics).

The Pharos Lighthouse of (A)lexandria, Egypt

'**Alex and Ria** aren't being **fair, Ross**.'

The Great Pyramid of (G)iza, Egypt

Some **geezer** thinks he's built this **great pyramid** in **Egypt**.

The Great Pyramid is the oldest wonder, built more than 4,000 years ago, and is the only one that remains today. The others were either destroyed by man or earthquakes.

Hanging Gardens of (B)abylon, Iraq

There's a **baby lion** hanging about in the **garden**. Gulp!

The Mausoleum at (H)alicarnassus, Turkey

Holly can ask us but **more so Liam**.

The Temple of Artemis at (E)phesus, Turkey

'Do you ever give **art a miss**?'
'N**ever, sis**.'

The Colossus of (R)hodes, Greece

The **colossal** statue towered over the **roads**.

The Statue of Zeus at (O)lympia, Greece

I wa**s use**less at the **Olympics** and froze like a **statue**.

FRENCH WORDS

There are three things you need to know about a French word — its meaning, how it's pronounced and how it's spelled. This category covers the first two but doesn't help with the spelling. Well, two out of three ain't bad! Here's a small selection of words that might help you with your French homework.

bike – (le) vélo

'On yer **bike**, dear **fellow**!'

bird – (le) oiseau

That **bird**'s singing **was oh**-so beautiful.

black – noire

The **Noire** Valley is **black** at night-time.

blue – bleu

'Which group do you prefer, **Blue** or **Blur**?'

---

building – (le) bâtiment

Batty men jump from **buildings**.

---

chicken – (le) poulet

'Oi, Miss **Chicken**! Don't lay a **poo** … **lay** an egg!'

---

countryside – (la) campagne

'Can we **camp on yer land**, Old MacDonald?'

day – (le) demain

Der man works all **day.**

dog – (le) chien

She yaps like a **dog**.

to eat – manger

Is blanc**mange a** horrible thing **to eat**?

egg – (le/un) oeuf

'Don't **egg** him on too much! **Enough** is enough.'

exercise book – (le) cahier

'Yippee-**ki-ay (cahier)**! Sir's lost our **exercise books**!'

hedgehog – (le) hérisson

There's a **hedgehog** on the **horizon (hérisson)**!

horse – (le) cheval

To scoop up a **horse**'s number twos, use a **shovel**.

hot or warm – chaud

This is one **hot show**!

kitchen – (la) cuisine

Quizzing your parent's **kitchen** skills is a bad idea.

to leave – partir

'De**part here**, if you want to **leave**.'

Monday – lundi

Lundi mundi

party – (la) boum

The music at the **party** went **boom** boom.[1]

pitch – (le) terrain

It's going **to rain** on the **pitch**.

---

to punish – punir

'Fido, if you **poo near** me, I'll **punish** you!'

---

pupil – (le/la) élève

Sometimes a **pupil** takes the **Eleven** Plus exam.

---

ready – prêt

Ready, pret … go!

---

road – (la) rue

So many **road**s… Which is the best **rou**te to take?

---

rubber or eraser – (la) gomme

Rubber gum

school – (la) école

'Has **A. Cole** been to **school**?'

shoes – (les) chaussures

'**Show sir's** face in your shiny **shoes**.'
'Yes, Sergeant!'

shower – (la) douche

Do 'shhhhh' continuously to sound like a **shower**.

sister – (la) soeur

<u>Si</u>ste<u>r</u>

sock – (la) chaussette

Right, the **show-set** is ready to **sock** it to 'em!

son – (le) fils

'What's the school **fee, son**?'

spider – (la) araignée

'Incy wincy **spider**, climbing up the spout. Down came **the rain** and washed the spider out.'[1]

ticket – (le) billet

A **BA ticket** (BA stands for British airways).

today – aujourd'hui

'Let's do it **today – or should we** do it some other time?'

town – (la) ville

A small **town** is a **vill**age.

Tuesday – mardi

Muddy shoes day.

water – (la) eau

'**Oh, what a** (**eau water**) b**eau**tiful morning…'

Wednesday – mercredi

'Get the **Merc ready**. I'm getting **wed next day**!'

wool – (la) laine

'Baa baa black sheep, have you any **wool**?
… And one for the little boy who lives down the **lane**.'

yes – oui

'Do you need a **wee**?'
'**Yes, we** do.'

[1] These links were created by Tom Dawson, Berkshire.

COMMONLY MISSPELLED WORDS

The definition of literacy is 'the ability to read and write', and linking can really help people with reading and writing. If U R A natural speller, it shouldn't take much effort. But usually it takes a lot of practice – or should that be alot of practise?

A lot is written alot a lot of the time. There is a space between the two words. See if you can put a lot and space together to create a familiar expression that will remind you of the space. Can you think of a link? Pat yourself on the back if you came up with a lot of space.

Now this practice/practise doobry is a dilemma.

Do I leave Emma? That's my **dilemma**.

The noun practi<u>c</u>e is spelled with a <u>c</u> and the verb practi<u>s</u>e has an <u>s</u>. If you take a peek inside these words, you'll see a different word in each one that will give you the link:

Practice has the word *ice* in it, which, more often than not, is a **noun** – for example, a block of ice.

Practise has the word *is* in it, which is a **verb**.

Spotted it!

Finding a word inside another word is not only fun but also a nice technique to aid your spelling. See what you can discover inside this tricky bunch, which are often misspelled:

apparent	argument	believe
category	chocolate	clothes
criticize	different	flood
instinct	laundry	Leicester
library	medicine	orange
orchestra	parliament	pregnant
rehearse	reminiscent	revenge
sharpening	twelfth	vegetable

These six are hiding two words together:

business	leisure	pleasure
sausage	separate	treasure

And these contain words spelled backwards (Hint: one uses every letter of the word!):

Wednesday	itinerary	stressed

155

It doesn't matter if the word is backwards. Your brain will store a little reminder that there is a word inside another word. And you will quickly work out whether it's forwards or backwards.

Answers:

One word:

1 ap**parent**   **2** ar**gum**ent   **3** be**lie**ve   **4** cat**egory**

5 cho**cola**te   **6** clo**thes**   **7** **critic**ize   **8** **differ**ent

9 f**loo**d   **10** inst**inct**   **11** la**undry**   **12** Lei**ce**ster

13 li**brar**y   **14** **medic**ine   **15** o**range**   **16** or**chest**ra

17 par**liam**ent   **18** preg**nant**   **19** reh**ears**e   **20** re**mini**scent

21 **reven**ge   **22** shar**pen**ing   **23** tw**elf**th   **24** ve**get**able

Two words:

25 **busin**ess (bus in)   **26** lei**sure**   (I sure)

27 ple**asure** (a sure)   **28** s**ausage** (a usage)

156

Once you've found the word, you're nearly there. All you need to do is put it into a sentence to make it memorable. Give it a go! After all, linking is about creating an image that works for you.

Here are some suggestions for you to salute or give the boot:

2 An ar**gum**ent over some **gum**? Now that's silly.

3 This is one **lie** you have to be**lie**ve.[1]

4 People with an **ego** don't like to be put into a cat**ego**ry.

5 Cho**cola**te-flavoured **Cola**? Yuck!

10 My ins**tinc**t told me I would like Monsters **Inc**.

157

15 My Orange mobile phone just rang.[2]

18 'Hey, Nan, I'm pregnant!'

19 My ears hurt when loud bands rehearse.

20 Are <u>recent</u> Minis <u>reminiscent</u> of the original cars?

23 …and when the clock struck for the twelfth time, an elf appeared.

24 'Go and get the vegetables!'

26 I sure love my leisure time!

28 Sausage is a usage for pork.

27 and **30** Discovering treasure is a sure pleasure.

34 We're stressed because someone has stolen our desserts!

The tricky letter in sep**a**rate is the first a, so you can include it in a few words:

a) You sep**arate a rat** from the rest of the class.
b) **A para**graph se**para**tes sentences.
c) 'Ma and **Pa** have a se**pa**rate bedroom from me.'

Staying on the parent theme for a second...

The nice thing about *parliament* is that it contains the word ***parent*** with the name ***Liam*** inside it. You can easily put this into a sentence.

If you put the two links ***Pa*** and ***parent*** back to back, you get one of the other words in the list, ***apparent***. This may not have been *obvious* to you (*obvious* is the meaning of *apparent*).

WHAT'S IN A WORD?

I'm always looking for words inside other words. But the fun doesn't stop there, my knight in the making! There are many other tell-tale signs in a word to help you remember its spelling. Let's take a look at this horrible-looking lot:

1 a**cc**ident   **2** marve**ll**ous   **3** vet**er**inary   **4** thr**ew**
5 confection**er**y

> These words can all be tricky little customers to spell - until now, that is!

1 They caught the a**cc**ident on **CC**TV.

2 What a marve**ll**ous **pair** of legs. (**ll** looks like a pair of legs, and **ll** = 2)

3 Is there an **E**mergency **R**oom (**ER**) in a vet**erina**ry hospital?

4 'I thr**ew** the ball from **e**ast to **w**est.'

5 Confection**e**ry contains **E** numbers.

> As you can see, letters often represent something in everyday life. This is good news because the easiest links to recall are the ones we can immediately relate to.

I C Y U R gr8

Some letters and numbers make the same sound as words, which can be extremely useful when linking. These are often used in text messaging:

B = be/bee
C = see/sea
I = eye/aye
Q = cue/queue
R = are
T = tea/tee
U = you/ewe
Y = why

1 = won
2 = to/too
4 = for/fore
8 = ate/hate. Add gr – gr8 = great

Have a play with them, and think of links to help you spell these slippery customers (the tricky bits are highlighted):

1 course   2 cuckoo   3 driving licence
4 favourite   5 fruit   6 much
7 picture   8 success

Close UR Is B4 U C my suggestions and think of a link. Y not? I 1der if U R a natural?

'Close your eyes before you see my suggestions and think of a link. Why not? I wonder if you are a natural?'

1 'Of co**ur**se U R!'

2 'Now **U C** me, now you don't!' says Mr C**uc**koo.

3 You need **2 C** to obtain a driving li**cenc**e.

4 '**U R** my favo**ur**ite.'

5 'U and I ought to eat fr**ui**t.'

6 U C m**uc**h better with your eyes open.

7 'Take **UR** pict**ur**e!'

8 It's great **2 C** su**cc**ess.

Double trouble

Double letters in a word can be a problem because they usually make the same sound as a single letter. Let's look at these fiddly four and see what we can come up with:

1 a**nn**iversary **2** di**sapp**ear
3 di**sapp**oint **4** emba**rrass**

1 'My parents are off to **Dublin (double N)** for their wedding a**nn**iversary.'

2 and **3** '**2P** or not **2P**? That i**S** the question.' Shakespeare never dis**app**oints and will never dis**app**ear.

4 That's **doubly** emba**rras**sing!

Here are a couple more spelling links that combine text language with a linking technique:

*C**olour*** (This is often misspelled because the sound of the word is nothing like its spelling.)

'What c**olour** are **Ur** eyes (**o o**)?' (Two Os look like two eyes.)

*Feb**ruary***

'R U a romantic like me?'

> This is assuming that you know that Valentine's Day is in February.

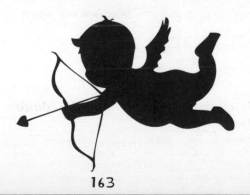

163

Here's another way to link a word that sounds different from the way it's spelled: put it inside a word which makes you sound out every syllable.

Here's a list of troublesome words (the bit in brackets shows how they're pronounced):

design (dee-zine)
reduce (ree-juice)
regime (ray-jeem)
reign (rane)
sign (sine)

Now ignore how each word is pronounced, and sound out the letters instead: D-E-S-I-G-N. Then put each word into another word which is pronounced the way it's spelled:

designate
reduction
regiment
reignite
signature

Breaking the law

There are many rules in the English language but there is always an exception to the rule. Take this one, for example:

*I before E, except after C (br**ie**f and re**cei**ve).*

It's a catchy link because it's a rhyming couplet, but unfortunately there are many exceptions. The rule should really be:

I before E except after C, as long as it's pronounced as a long E.

But this is too much of a mouthful, so there's less chance of you remembering it. You also have to explain what a *long E* is (pronounced *ee*). This has the opposite effect of a memory aid and what it stands for. And even if you do manage to remember this extended rule, there are still a few exceptions! The solution is to *think of a link* for these bad boys.

Seize and *weird* are two words that live outside the letter of the law.

Seize

Se**ize** the pr**ize**!

Weird

That b**ird** looks we**ird**.

You feel a whole lot better when linking a letter!

The links for *seize* and *weird* use the *letter linking* technique – where you link the tricky letter(s) with the same letter(s) in another word in a familiar expression.

Your brain stores away many thousands of expressions and they're usually easy to remember: *bread and butter, pull your trousers up, join in, football pitch, remote control*. We can use these phrases to help with spelling.

See if you can *letter link* these words (the awkward letters are in bold):

1 anc**ho**r

2 b**us**y

3 b**ut**cher

4 **c**ent**re**

5 **c**om**e**

6 co**mmit**ment

7 cres**c**ent

8 crum**b**

9 ex**hilar**ate

10 fishm**o**nger

11 ga**rag**e

12 han**d**some

13 int**err**upt

14 Lond**o**n

15 Medi**terr**anean

16 mus**cle**

17 ne**cess**ary

18 o**ppor**tunity

19 po**rrid**ge

20 sec**ret**ary

21 swe**a**t

22 w**h**ack

23 **w**rap

1 An an**chor**'s **ho**ok.

2 **Busy bus**

3 B**ut**chers c**ut** meat.

4 The cen**tre** is the **core**.

5 '**Come home**.'

6 With com**mit**ment, you can get to the su**mmit** of anything.

7 A cres**cent** is **C**-shaped.

8 **B**readcrum**b**

9 That was **hilar**ious yet ex**hilar**ating.

10 Fishm**o**ngers p**ong**.

11 A ga**rag**e mechanic's **rag.**

12 Hand**some** **d**evil

13 'Don't inter**r**upt Uncle **Terr**y!'

14 London Z**oo**

15 'Uncle **Terr**y's won a Medi**terr**anean cruise!'

16 Mr Mus**cl**e: a **cl**eaning agent.

17 Listening in **cl**ass is ne**c**e**ss**ary.

18 'I will su**pport** you at every o**pport**unity.'

19 **H**o**rr**id po**rr**idge.

20 'My **secret**ary says she's called Jo, but **secret**ly she's called M<u>ary</u>.'

21 Armpits swe<u>at</u>.

22 **Wh**ack and **h**it.

23 **W**rap up **w**arm.

The letters don't have to be in order for letter linking to work. As long as you know the letters appear somewhere in the word, then common sense takes over.

Here are three examples:

O<u>ccu</u>r
Cracks o**ccu**r in old age.

O<u>cca</u>sion
The **soc**cer World Cup is a huge o**cca**sion.

A**ccom**plishment
Creating your own **com**i**c** is an a**ccom**plishment

My personal best (PB) for the longest letter link is six letters. See if you can beat it. It's for remembering how many Cs and Ms there are in the word <u>recommend</u>:

'I re**commen**d you read my **commen**ts in your school report.'

If you're not sure how many Ms there are in *comment*, then remember that the only common words that begin with *com* followed by a vowel are: com**a**, com**e**, com**e**dy, com**e**t and com**i**c. The rest all have a consonant as the fourth letter.

SIR LINKALOT'S TIP

Using crumb and commitment as two
examples, go online and type in a
search engine:

a) Definition of crumb

When you find a dictionary website, look
for the definition of crumb. At the end,
you should find words related to crumb
that have a B in them somewhere. This is
where I found breadcrumb!

b) Words containing mmit

Some websites list words containing any
combination of letters you want. When
you find one of these sites, look at the
list of words that have 'mmit' in them
that you can link to commitment. This is
where I found summit.

These word searches are an excellent
way of using the Internet to help you
learn.

170

'The CIA is special, Mr Bond.'

Did you know that all words ending -cian are jobs?
Here's a selection:

beauti**cian**   diete**cian**   electri**cian**   magi**cian**
mathemati**cian**

musi**cian**   opti**cian**   politi**cian**   physi**cian**
techni**cian**

James Bond works for the British Secret Intelligence Service
(SIS), aka MI6. The American version of James Bond works
for the CIA (Central Intelligence Agency). The people listed
above work for a company and have a company (the CIA)
inside their name!

One of the reasons the <u>CIA</u> is special is that it's in the word
'spe<u>cia</u>l'. And if you haven't heard of the CIA, just remember
that it's a <u>C</u>ompany <u>I</u>n <u>A</u>merica.

Another fun task is trying to find words that are wholly made
up of other smaller words. This can help with spelling.

cardboard: card board

caterpillar: cater pillar

cupboard: cup board

extraordinary: extra ordinary

incubated: in Cuba Ted

medallion: medal lion

repertoire: re per to I re

together: to get her

tomorrow: Tom or row

wardrobe: ward robe

If you can think of any others, then send them to www.thinkalink.co.uk where you'll find thousands more spelling links.

Let's finish off this spelling section with links for all sorts of words:

abbreviation BBC is an abbreviation.

archaeologist Arch rivals of archaeologist Indiana Jones often ended up in A & E.

association The **SIS** and **CIA** are spy asso**cia**tions.

autumn Does **aut**umn begin in **Au**gust and end in November?

beautiful Be a **bea**utiful person.

because ...be**cause a use** for linking is helping you to spell.

blew The wind b**lew** from **e**ast to **w**est.

breakfast Breakfast charges my personal **AA** batteries.

calendar Lend a hand at Christmas (ca**lenda**r).

calm, placid Calm, placid

chicken Chicken and **e**gg

column a) Newspaper colum**n** b) **N**elson's Colum**n**

conqueror Was William the Conqu**ero**r a h**ero**?

corridor 'The wallpaper in that **corrid**or is h**orrid**!'

desert a) Desert sand b) Sahara Desert

environment There's pressure **on men** and women to create a green envir**onmen**t.

every I get excited **every** Christmas **Eve**.

exciting Xmas (Christmas) is so ex**cit**ing!

exercise You **exert** energy when you **exer**cise.

friend When **Fri**day ends, I see my **fri**ends.

government So who does **govern** the **govern**ment?

guess U **guess**ed it!

handkerchief **Hand**kerchief

heroes Kiss the feet and **toes** of your her**oes.**

illiterate 'Wi**ll it** be a problem if I'm **illit**erate?'

isle The **Isle** of Man **is left** of England.

jewellery I saw some beautiful jew**ellery** advertised in *ELLE* magazine.

kitchen The eggs of a **hen** are kept in the kit**chen**.

laugh We always have a la**ugh** in **Aug**ust.

lavatory 'Is there **a story** explaining why the lav**atory** chain is broken?'

loose (adjective) A loose **loo se**at.

lose (verb) **Los**s **los**e

magnificent What a magnificent **ice** cream!

minuscule You score A **minus** for this link, as their is a **minus**cule error.
(Can you spot the deliberate mistake in this link?)

Mississippi **Miss is sipp**ing some fresh water.

nuisance Spelling *nuisance* **is a** nui**s**ance.

once **On**ce up**on** a time…

oven St**ove** and **oven**

parallel In a **rall**y, cars cross the pa**rall**el lines in the middle of the road. So there's only **one L** (loser) at the end.

parent Parents **are** always right!

pavilion There's a cricket wicket (**III**) in the pavilion. (**ili** looks like the three stumps that make up a wicket.)

pencil Pencil **case**

penguin **G**, **U in** this country? Surely not, Mr Pen**guin**![4]

people a) People **eat o**melettes. **P**eople love **e**ggs. b) **P**eople **e**mail **o**ther **p**eople lovely **e**mails.

permanent A lion, with its striking **mane**, is a per**mane**nt threat.

persistence With persis**tence**, you'll get **ten** out of ten in your spelling test.

pharaoh 'Sun god **Ra** was the patron of the pha**ra**ohs.'
'**Oh**.'

phone '**P**hone **ho**me.'

piece Pie**ce** of **pie**

pier **Pie** and chips on the **pie**r.

plane Planes land.

plain 'In plain English please…'

plumber 'Dad, have you got the n**umber** for the pl**umber**?'

pursue I pursue U.

receipt 'Is this piece (**eceip** backwards) of paper the **receip**t?'

receive 'Yes, yes, **I've** received it!'[5]

reduce **Reduc**e your speed when **U C** a **red** light.

refrigerator 'An ice-cool **ref rig** a match? Never!'

reindeer Red-nosed **re**indeer

relevant/relevance What's the re**levan**ce of a navel? (navel = **levan** backwards)

rhythm Rhythm helps your two hips move.

said 'Say again? I didn't hear what you said.'

satellite Sate**ll**ite **telly**

saucer 'Why is there **an u**pturned **c**up on that s**auc**er?'

silhouette Sil**houe**tte: take the 's' (for shadow) out of the word 'house'.

skilful a) W**ilf** is sk**ilf**ul.
  b) Some footballers are so sk**ilful,** they could play on one leg (**l**).

soldier Sol**di**ers **die** in battle.

suit '**U** and **I** s**ui**t each other.'

swimming a) M&M's are swi**mm**ing in calories
b) Millimetres (**mm**) decide a swi**mm**ing race.

temperature Temp**era**tures are rising in the modern **era**.

theatre Going to the the**atre** is **a tre**at.

there, where and here 'W**here** – **here** or **t**h**ere**?'[6]

thought and through '**O U** grizzly **h**edgehog! You haven't th**ough**t this road-crossing strategy thr**ough**.'

178

thousand Sand is made up of thou**sand**s of grains.

trouble 'O, U are in so much tr**ou**ble!'

tyre Y R ty**re**s rubber?

uncontrollable A **roll**ing stone is uncont**roll**able.

wasp A **wasp** and an **asp** sting.

wriggle Worms wriggle.

xylophone X and Y together make a Z sound.

yacht Being on a **yach**t gives me a head**ach**e.

young Young people say '**Yo**!'

And finally, here are some links for the most commonly misspelled word in the English language:

accommodate/accommodation

a) 'What are the Cheshire Cat (**CC**), Mickey Mouse (**MM**) and Scooby <u>Doo</u> doing in my a**ccommo**dation?'
b) 'I'd love **2 C** if the **O2** Arena could a**ccommo**date the world's supply of **M&M**'s.'

Not one, not two but three!

So far, you might have come across a fairly uncommon species called a double link – a link that helps you remember two things at once. Now brace yourselves for an extremely rare breed indeed – the triple link.

The word in question is Britain.

On first viewing, you may wonder what's so special about one common word. However, if you start to look inside the word, some magic links start to reveal themselves. These three links can help you remember two facts about Britain, and how to spell the word itself!

Link number one:

Fingers on buzzers… General-knowledge question no. 1:

Which is the longest road in Britain?

The M1, M6, M25 or A1?

I'll give you a clue – the answer is in BRIT**AI**N…

Yep, it's the A1, running from London all the way to Edinburgh in Scotland – 660 kilometres in fact!

180

Link number two:

General knowledge question no. 2:

Which is the highest mountain in Britain?

The answer is Ben Nevis (Scotland), whose initials (BN) are at the beginning and the end of **B**RITAI**N**.

Link number three:

Spelling quiz time!

How do you spell 'Britain'?

Now you know that you know the A1 runs through Britain, it will help you spell the word 'Britian': it reminds you that the ending is **_ain_** not *ian* or *ern*.

---

[1] This link was created by Alan Bigley, Hertfordshire.

[2] This link was created by Lulu Salmon, Ruby Weston and Anna Simonetti, East Sussex.

[3] This link was created by Claire Adams, West Sussex.

[4] This link was created by Freddie Salmon, East Sussex.

[5] This link was created by Bethy Reeves, London.

Certain letters of the alphabet sound alike over the phone, such as A and H, and B and V. To avoid confusion, a phonetic alphabet is used by the police, emergency services and the army. It works by using specific words to represent each letter of the alphabet. Each letter is given a code word.

A for Alpha

A for **alpha**bet.

abcde

B for Bravo

a) 'I'll give you a **B** for that opera-singing… **Bravo!**'
b) '**Be brave, oh (bravo)**, little one.' [1]

C for Charlie

C for **Charlie**, **C** for **Chaplin**.

SEE?

D for Delta

That D grade **dealt a** (**delta**) major blow to my university prospects.

E for Echo

'It's **echoey** (**E**) in here.' 'What?' 'I said it's echoey in here!' 'What?' [1]

F for Foxtrot

'**If** (**F**) that **fox trot**s off with another chicken…' [1]

G for Golf

'**Gee,** that's a long **golf** shot!'[1]

H for Hotel

Oh, tell (h**otel**) me the link, I'm **itch**ing (**aitching**) to know!

I for India

Don't poke me **in de ear** or de **eye** (**I**).

J for Juliet

A **jay** perched on my **Juliet** balcony.[1]

K for Kilo

My **K**9 (canine) weighs 50 **kilo**s![1]

L for Lima

Eliminate (**L Lima**nate) the problem.[1]

M for Mike

'Now I've got the **mike**, I don't know what to say! **Mmm**…'[1]

N for November

No ember remained alight after Bonfire **N**ight.[1]

O for Oscar

O, I've just won an **Oscar**!

P for Papa

'**Papa** won the Largest Vegetable competition with a **pea**!'[1]

Q for Quebec

The **queue** (**Q**) for the **Quebec** flight took hours!

R for Romeo

'**Romeo**, Romeo, wherefore **ar**t (**R**) thou Romeo?'

S for Sierra

Give **sea air a** try. **S**'good for you.[1]

T for Tango

I prefer to drink **Tango** rather than **tea**.

U for Uniform

a) 'Why aren't **U** wearing your **uniform**?'
b) 'The policeman in **uniform** arrested **U**.'[1]

V for Victor

Winston Churchill's legendary '**V** for **Victory**' salute.

W for Whisky

There are more slopes in the letter **W** than any other.
So what do we do? **We ski**!

X for X-ray

X-ray spe**c**s (**X**)[1]

Y for Yankee

Why (**Y**) is an American called a **Yankee**?

> ## Why is an American called a Yankee?
> There are many different stories about where the word Yankee comes from, but this is my favourite:
>
> When Dutch settlers arrived in America in the 1600s, New York was called New Amsterdam. The English, who arrived later on, rudely called the Dutch 'John Cheese' because they were famous for their cheese. The Dutch translation of John Cheese is Jan Kaas (pronounced Yahn-Kees). And that explains the term Yankee!

Z for Zulu

Animals use **zee zoo loo**.[2]

---

[1] This link was created by Claire Adams, West Sussex.

[2] This link was created by Alan Newell, Berkshire.

Two-dimensional SHAPES (how many sides?)

Here are some links to remember the number of sides in each 2D shape. (NB: squares and rectangles are quadrilaterals.)

3 sides – triangle
Try angling. It's a **free (3)** sport.

4 sides – quadrilateral
A **quad** bike has **4** wheels.

5 sides – pentagon
A **pent**house offers **5**-star luxury.

6 sides – hexagon
Si**x** and he**x**agon.

7 sides – heptagon
The **seven** dwarfs **helped again (heptagon)**.

8 sides – octagon
I just **ate (8) oct**opus and I h**ate**d it!

9 sides – nonagon
<u>Ni</u>ne and <u>no</u>nagon.

10 sides – decagon
Where's my **Double Decker** gone? Have you ca**ten** it?

11 sides – hendecagon
Wouldn't it be great to see a huge **hen deck a** football team, all **11** of them?

12 sides – dodecagon
Do deck the house in preparation for the **12** Days of Christmas.

THE MR. MEN

Mr. Men is a series of **46** children's books by Roger Hargreaves. The first book in the series is Mr. Tickle. It's about a small round figure with long, bendy arms and an urge to tickle anyone within reach.

Here are some links for the first ten Mr. Men books:

1. Mr. Tickle
a) **Tickle** every**one**.[1]
b) **Tick all** the boxes to be number **one**.

2. Mr. Greedy
Having a **second** helping is **greedy**.

3. Mr. Happy
a) **Happy** days … I'm **free**!
b) Don't worry, **three happy**.

4. Mr. Nosey
Do **nosey**-parkers join the police **4**ce?

5. Mr. Sneeze

Put your **hand** over your mouth when you **sneeze**. (Hand = **5** digits.)

6. Mr. Bump

Ouch! That **bump** hit me for **six**.

7. Mr. Snow

Snow White and the **Seven** Dwarfs.

8. Mr. Messy

I **8 mess**.

9. Mr. Topsy-Turvy

If you turn him **upside down**, he looks like a **9**.

10. Mr. Silly

Tennis and **ten** pin bowling are **silly** sports.

[1] This link was created by Aryan Mishra, London.

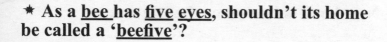

* As a <u>bee</u> has <u>five eyes</u>, shouldn't its home be called a '<u>beefive</u>'?

~~~~~~~~~~~~~~~~

* You'd be a <u>fool</u> to write '-full' not '<u>-ful</u>' at the end of a word.

~~~~~~~~~~~~~~~~

* David <u>Tennant</u> was Doctor Who number <u>ten</u>.[1]

~~~~~~~~~~~~~~~~

* Disney<u>land</u> is near <u>LA</u> (Los Angeles), California, and Disney W<u>or</u>ld is in Fl<u>or</u>ida.[1]

~~~~~~~~~~~~~~~~

* You don't have to be <u>James</u> <u>Bond</u> to work out that the international dialling code for Russia is <u>007</u>!

✳ **Neil <u>A</u>rmstrong, <u>B</u>uzz Aldrin and Michael <u>C</u>ollins were the first astronauts to land on the Moon.**

✳ **New York is known as the Big Apple.**

Is a GranNY Smith a big apple?

✳ **Father's Day is celebrated on the third Sunday of June.**

The third letter of Su**n**day, Ju**n**e and ma**n** is **N**.
(Mother's Day/Mothering Sunday is the fourth Sunday of Lent in Easter, so the date varies each year.)

✳ **Edward the Confessor (1042–1066) ruled just before William the Conqueror (1066–1087).**

Confessor comes before *conqueror* in the dictionary.

* **African elephants' ears are bigger than those of Indian elephants.**

Africa is bigger than India.

~~~~~~~~~~~~~~~~~~~~~~~~~~~~~~~~~~~~~~

* **Edward Teach was the real name of the infamous pirate Blackbeard.**

'Does your **'ed teach**er have a **blackbeard**?'

~~~~~~~~~~~~~~~~~~~~~~~~~~~~~~~~~~~~~~

* **Cape Horn is found at the bottom of South America.**

Chile, where Cape Horn is located, is horn shaped.

~~~~~~~~~~~~~~~~~~~~~~~~~~~~~~~~~~~~~~

* **In a fraction, the denominator is the bottom number.**

A **demon** is at the **bottom** of the Earth. [2]

✳ **The Tropic of Cancer is in the northern hemisphere and the Tropic of Capricorn in the southern hemisphere.**

You hold a **can** in your hand (the top part of your body) and you get **corn**s on your foot (the bottom part).

~~~~~~

✳ The **solstices** are in the **summer** and **winter**, when the Sun is directly over the **Tropic of Cancer** (summer) and the **Tropic of Capricorn** (winter). They are the two times in the year when the Sun reaches its highest or lowest point in the sky at noon, marked by the longest and shortest days.

An **equinox** happens **twice a year** (about 20 March and 22 September), when the Sun crosses the **equator** and day and night are of equal length.

Solstice: **sol** means **Sun** and **ice** is winter.
Sols**tic**e contains a **T** for **Tropic** and a **C** for **Cancer** and **Capricorn**.

Equinox has no T or C. So this must be when the Sun is directly over the **equ**ator in the spring and autumn.

✷ Burn's Night in Scotland is celebrated on 25 January.

It's a month after Christmas (**25 January**), and Santa's still feeling those chimney **burns**.

~~~~~~

✷ The Dolomites mountain range is in Italy.

Dolom**it**es – **It**aly

~~~~~~

✷ Charles Darwin is on the back of a ten-pound note.

'Congratulations, **Charles**, you've just got **ten** out of ten in your test. You're **Darwin**ner!'

★ Beethoven wrote nine symphonies.

One symphony for each letter of his name.

~~~~~~~~~~~~~~~~~~~~~~~~~~~~~~~

★ The North Pole is in the Arctic Ocean and the South Pole is in the Antarctic.

You look **up** at an **arc** and **down** at an **ant**.[3]

~~~~~~~~~~~~~~~~~~~~~~~~~~~~~~~

★ The number pi (∏) to six decimal places is 3.141592.

The number of letters in each word in the following sentence corresponds to a digit:

How (3) I (1) wish (4) I (1) could (5) calculate (9) pi (2).

~~~~~~~~~~~~~~~~~~~~~~~~~~~~~~~

★ The Grand Canyon can be found in the US state Arizona.

'Cor, is this **Grand Canyon** an **arid zone or** what?' (Arid means dry.)

✱ **The Cape of Good Hope is in South Africa.**

South African Nelson Mandela was a **good** man who brought **hope** to the nation.

~~~~~~

✱ **The Beaufort Scale measures windspeed.**

Blowfort

~~~~~~

✱ **Chiropractors specialize in treating back problems.**

Cairo, the ancient capital city of Egypt, goes **back** a long way.

~~~~~~

✱ **You can get the disease scurvy, if you don't have enough Vitamin C.**

a) Sailors used to get **scurvy** at **sea** (**C**).
b) The letter C**'s curvy**.

* **Scandinavia is made up of the kingdoms of Sweden, Norway and Denmark.**

Sca**ND**inavia – **S**weden, **N**orway, **D**enmark.

---

* **Lord Horatio Nelson lost his right arm and the sight in his right eye.**

Eye **A**rm **R**ight (I am right)! (The first letters of **E**ye **A**rm **R**ight spell 'ear'.)

---

* **Mount Everest is the world's highest mountain.**

If you **ever rest** on the top of this monster, you'll see some great views.

---

* **The Leaning Tower of Pisa is in Italy.**

The leaning tower of **pizza**.

✳ Per cent means divided by 100.

The percent symbol **%** looks like a diagonal **1** and **two zeros (00)**.

~~~~~~~~~~~~~~~~~~~~~~~~~~~~~~~~~~~~~~~

✳ The Aztec people were from Mexico.

Aztecs rhymes with **Mex**.

~~~~~~~~~~~~~~~~~~~~~~~~~~~~~~~~~~~~~~~

✳ *Entomology* means the study of insects, but *etymology* means the study of words.

antomology and (l)**etter**mology

~~~~~~~~~~~~~~~~~~~~~~~~~~~~~~~~~~~~~~~

✳ In geology, stala<u>ctites</u> hang down from the ceiling and stala<u>gmites</u> grow up from the ground.

a) Loose **tights (tites)** fall down, little **mites** grow up.[4]
b) stala**c**tites: c = ceiling; stala**g**mites: g = ground.

✳ Which months have 31 days?

a) '30 days have September,
April, June and November.
All the rest have 31,
Except for February alone,
Which has 28 days clear,
And 29 in each leap year.'

b) Make your hands into fists and put them together. Starting at the knuckle of your left little finger, touch each knuckle and the gap between each knuckle, counting off the months of the year as you go. The first knuckle is January, the first gap is February, and so on.

<u>Each month which you count on a knuckle has 31 days.</u>

~~~~~~

✳ Which way do you tighten a nut?

Right = tight, left = loose.

~~~~~~

✳ We usually have 32 teeth (including wisdom teeth).

'My **dental** appointment is at **2.30** (tooth hurty) (2 + 30 = **32**).'

* **The first person to swim the English Channel was Matthew Webb in 1875.**

Most **18**-year-olds spend **three quarters** (**75** per cent) of their time surfing the **Web**, and the rest **channel**-hopping.

---

* **A sonnet is a 14-line poem.**

'I'm off to **sun it** (**sonnet**) up on my **14**-day summer holiday…'

---

* **St George's Day is celebrated on 23 April (23/4).**

'Just one dragon? Give me **2**, **3** or **4**. I'll slay 'em all!' brags **St George**.[5]

---

* **Scafell Pike, in Cumbria, is England's highest mountain.**

'I could cycle for **England** until I **fell** off my **mountain bike** (**pike**) and got a **scar**.'

✴ **Queen Victoria was born in 1819 and was crowned in 1837.**

Victoria was between **18** and **19** years old when she became Queen in **1837** (**18** + **19** = **37**).

~~~~~~

✴ **The order of the vowels is A, E, I, O, U.**

'**Eh (A)**! 'E and **I owe (O) you (U)** money.'

~~~~~~

✴ **Ruins of the Inca civilization are mainly found in Peru, South America.**

Peru Inca

[1] These links were created by Phil Isaac, Cornwall.

[2] This link was created by Jeannie Psomoulis, Australia.

[3] This link was created by Dominic O'Brien, Dorset (World Memory Champion).

[4] This link was created by Phil Stubbs, Derbyshire.

[5] This link was created by Alex McGrath, Berkshire.

WELL THAT JUST ABOUT COVERS IT...
FOR NOW!

I hope you've enjoyed the ride and, more importantly, got your head around linking and how powerful it can be - it can help you remember absolutely any fact you care to think of!

Don't forget, if you visit the website you can request a link for anything whatsoever, no matter how weird or wonderful it may be.

www.thinkalink.co.uk
is the website...

Will we link it? I think we might!

Pip pip!

Sir Linkalot

OUT NOW

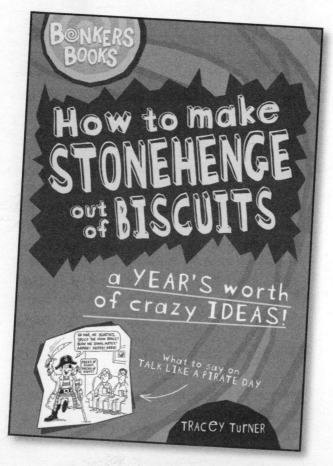